NEGOTIATE TO WIN!

TALKING YOUR WAY TO WHAT YOU WANT

Patrick Collins

author of *Speak with Power and Confidence*

STERLING

x

book

New York / London
www.sterlingpublishing.com

For Donna, Kristen, and Laura

STERLING and the distinctive Sterling logo are registered
trademarks of Sterling Publishing Co., Inc.

Library of Congress Cataloging-in-Publication Data

Collins, Patrick J.
  Negotiate to win! : talking your way to what you want / Patrick J. Collins.
    p. cm.
  Includes bibliographical references and index.
  ISBN 978-1-4027-6122-5 (hc-trade cloth : alk. paper)
  1. Negotiation in business. 2. Negotiation. I. Title.
  HD58.6.C65 2009
  658.4'052—dc22   2008028663

10 9 8 7 6 5 4 3 2 1

Published by Sterling Publishing Co., Inc.
387 Park Avenue South, New York, NY 10016
© 2009 by Patrick Collins
Distributed in Canada by Sterling Publishing
c/o Canadian Manda Group, 165 Dufferin Street
Toronto, Ontario, Canada M6K 3H6
Distributed in the United Kingdom by GMC Distribution Services
Castle Place, 166 High Street, Lewes, East Sussex, England BN7 1XU
Distributed in Australia by Capricorn Link (Australia) Pty. Ltd.
P.O. Box 704, Windsor, NSW 2756, Australia

Manufactured in the United States of America
All rights reserved

Sterling ISBN 978-1-4027-6122-5

For information about custom editions, special sales, premium and
corporate purchases, please contact Sterling Special Sales
Department at 800-805-5489 or specialsales@sterlingpublishing.com.

Contents

Chapter Ten: Cross-Cultural Negotiations ······ 131

Chapter Eleven: When Negotiations Fail ······ 145

Introduction

Negotiate to Win! is a complete tactical guide to the information and interpersonal tools you need to become a master negotiator. From the words you use and the strategies you employ to the people skills you need to make things go your way, *Negotiate to Win!* shows you how to speak up and get what you want.

If you have ever walked away from a business negotiation and said, "Next time I'll do better," you need *Negotiate to Win!* If you have ever said, "There's no point in negotiating, they'll only say no," *Negotiate to Win!* will show you how to rid yourself of that very costly mind-set. If you have ever avoided negotiation because you were afraid of failure or rejection, *Negotiate to Win!* will dispel those fears and empower you.

Most books on negotiation take one of two approaches. The first is what I call the "abracadabra" approach. Its proponents claim that by saying the magic words, or precisely the right thing at the right time, you can talk your way to total victory in *every* situation *every* time. If that were true, negotiation strategies would be unnecessary and all you would need is a list of magic words to achieve your objective.

The other treatment of negotiation is the "case-study" approach, or what I call the if-it-worked-for-them-it-just-might-work-for-you approach. The theory here is that you can apply information from and analyses of various cases to your own attempts at negotiation. What case-study proponents fail to point out is that the results of one negotiation cannot consistently be used to predict what will happen in another negotiation or with another issue. No two negotiations are exactly alike. What works well in one session may fail miserably in another. As they say in the mutual fund industry, past results are not indicative of future performance.

Negotiation is both an art and a science. It's a science in the sense that there are principles, strategies, and rules, but it is a very imprecise science. In a laboratory, all the bottles are labeled; a scientist knows *exactly* what substances to mix in order to produce a specific reaction. People, including negotiators, don't come precisely labeled, so there can't be a clear prediction of what the mixture of strategies and personalities will produce. A fair offer to one person can seem like an outright swindle to another. What someone considers a legitimate question can be taken by another as a grievous insult. Unlike in the laboratory, the results at the negotiating table may be not only variable but highly unpredictable.

The infinite variables of human behavior—a multiplicity of personality traits, idiosyncrasies, and ranges of reactions—make for a wide array of possible outcomes. The artistry in negotiation comes in knowing when to apply which strategies to which people to maximize your chances for success. *Negotiate to Win!* helps you sort out the science and the art of negotiation, giving you the control you need to achieve a favorable outcome.

There are three elements in all negotiation encounters: (1) your ability as a negotiator, (2) management of the negotiation environment, and (3) tactics and strategies of negotiation. *Negotiate to Win!* tackles these elements with a three-pronged approach, telling you *exactly* what you need to know to achieve success in the art and science of negotiation.

The first part of *Negotiate to Win!*—"Building Your Personal Negotiating Power"—is about *you*. It teaches you how to build the attitude and outlook of a successful negotiator. An essential element in building the right mind-set is simply getting you to negotiate. *Negotiate to Win!* gets you started immediately with "guerrilla negotiation tactics," a series of effective and easily applied measures to get you negotiating right away. *Negotiate to Win!* even suggests a series of real-life situations in which you can negotiate but probably haven't—until now.

The second part of *Negotiate to Win!*—"Management Skills for Negotiators"—is about managing the negotiation environment, from the people you encounter to the language you use to the physical surroundings in which negotiations happen. Since disagreement is so often about people simply not listening to one another, *Negotiate to Win!* also includes a chapter on enhanced listening skills as a further means of sharpening your negotiating ability.

Part Three of *Negotiate to Win!*—"Advanced Tactics and Special Situations"—focuses on strategies and tactics you need when the issues are complex and the stakes are high. Since you may, at times, find yourself on the receiving end of these strategies, *Negotiate to Win!* offers a chapter on negotiation countermeasures to make certain that you don't become a victim of another skilled negotiator.

Negotiations are not always local. That's why *Negotiate to Win!* includes a chapter that covers the seldom considered but increasingly common matter of intercultural negotiation. This unique chapter gives you pointers on what to expect when negotiating with members of cultures other than your own. For example, time is considered more valuable in some cultures than it is in others. In some places, a simple inquiry about flight schedules might be mistaken for an expression of your distaste for spending time with a potential business partner. (You'll make your flight, but don't buy a return ticket because they won't be inviting you back.) *Negotiate to Win!* leads you through the intricacies of intercultural negotiation and away from the inadvertent but costly negotiating flubs that may await you in other lands. Don't leave home without it!

Another special situation is the impasse. Working your way through a deadlock requires a special set of skills and judgment calls covered in *Negotiate to Win!* Not only will you learn how to get things going again, but you'll learn when to walk away if that's the right move.

In the event that you are pressed for time but in need of a quick review, *Negotiate to Win!* wraps up with a summary chapter entitled "The Ten Commandments of Negotiation." When you need a quick refresher, these commandments not only present the absolute essentials for successful negotiation, but are also a kind of "lightning-round" review of the negotiation process.

With this three-pronged approach (covering the negotiator's mind-set, management tools for the negotiation environment, and advanced tactics and special situations), *Negotiate to Win!* is the most comprehensive guide to negotiation success available. Does this mean you'll win every time or get *exactly* what you want from every negotiation? Probably not. Just as knowing the melody and lyrics to "New York, New York," doesn't make you Frank Sinatra, knowing a few negotiation strategies won't make you a master negotiator. However, a thorough knowledge of what you can do better and the elimination of what you are doing wrong will vastly improve your ability to negotiate in *any* situation. With practice and the information contained in *Negotiate to Win!* you won't merely level the playing field; you'll tilt it very strongly in your direction.

Good luck and great negotiating!

PART ONE

Building Your Personal
Negotiating Power

CHAPTER ONE

Discovering the *Real* Meaning of Negotiation

AT-A-GLANCE SUMMARY
This chapter is about the nature of negotiation—a uniquely structured conversation geared toward gaining an advantage. You'll learn about the difference between negotiation and confrontation and when to use each. Also included are hints on building the *negotiation mentality* as well as the five secrets of successful negotiators.

What Is Negotiation?

Negotiation is different from any other type of conversation you'll ever have—different in two main ways from storytelling, information sharing, or just plain gossip. First, negotiation is structured to achieve a specific outcome, usually in the form of an agreement. Second, negotiation is the only form of conversation that carries with it the constant possibility of success or failure—meaning you might not get what you want or you may fail to reach an agreement at all. Success in negotiations can come only when you've learned to control the flow of conversation toward agreement and minimized your fear of failure.

The beginning of that success is rooted in understanding the *real* meaning of negotiation. There aren't any magic-bullet words that will pummel the other side into submission. Negotiation is about reaching agreement and, as you'll learn in the pages that follow, it's essentially the same activity whether the stakes are great or small.

Reaching agreement means you get what you want and the other person in the negotiation gets something in return. Maybe you'll do better than your counterpart will—maybe you'll gain an advantage—but in real negotiation, both sides feel that they are gaining something, which is the basis for each party's willingness to agree.

Successful negotiation has to be a win-win situation. For example, in the most bitter labor dispute, tempers may flare, sides may be very far apart, and there may be an ongoing strike. However, once negotiations conclude, neither side makes a victory statement.

Successful negotiation never ends in statements like "We really beat the daylights out of the other side." Instead, you'll hear statements such as "Both sides have worked out an agreement we believe to be fair to all of the parties, and we look forward to resuming work." These statements illustrate precisely what negotiation is about. Each side knows they gave something, but they also received something in return. The employees got a raise or better working conditions, and the company will pay wages it can afford and a contract that ensures a period of labor stability. The mutuality of the outcome is integral to its success.

What Negotiation Isn't

At the conclusion of a lecture on the win-win nature of negotiation, a member of my audience pointed out that if she had acted on my advice, she would still be at her auto dealer's service department. Instead, she had arrived in a loaner car—a car she had at first been denied after politely requesting it. Only after she verbally roughed up the service manager was the denial rescinded. My audience member made the frequently made mistake of confusing negotiation with confrontation. Confrontation, unlike negotiation, has a winner and loser.

Confrontation is an all-or-nothing situation. It can be appropriate and even useful when there won't be a next time, or when you can risk walking away with nothing, or when you are right and the other party is wrong. In situations like those, confrontation may be the only option, but it's always a risky option. When you confront, you've got to consider beforehand what you'll get if you win and also what it will cost you to lose.

Negotiation is about gaining an advantage and perhaps giving something in return, but unlike in confrontation, the successful negotiator *never* walks away empty-handed. In confrontation, the winner may gain an advantage, but, on the flip side, the loser may be left with a need to get even. The woman with the loaner car should have handled things differently. Sure, confrontation worked, but she probably had to wait five months for her next service appointment!

Especially if there is the possibility of a next time, negotiation is highly preferable to confrontation. Now that you're convinced that negotiation is worthwhile, it's time to convince you to negotiate!

Discovering Your Personal Negotiating Power

Everything Is Negotiable!

To become a successful negotiator, make your motto "Everything is negotiable." Before you can learn strategies and tactics, you've got to develop a mind-set that has you ready to negotiate at all times. You must learn to consider virtually *everything* negotiable. You also need to increase your willingness to engage others in negotiation. Your world is filled with signs that say "Negotiators Not Welcome." These signs come in the form of price tags, policy statements, disclaimers ("The management is not responsible for . . ."), and lines like "That's my final offer . . . take it or leave it!" Open a newspaper and you'll see classified ads with prices followed by the word "firm." Call that seller after an item has gone unsold for a week and you'll find that "firm" price has become quite squishy, or *highly* negotiable!

In addition to these signs, daily life presents all of us with a constant stream of situations that discourage negotiation by portraying us as rude or troublesome for trying to improve our situations. How often have you accepted a table near the door in a restaurant because you were hesitant to ask for a more desirable spot? Think about the time you checked into a hotel and learned that the *exact* accommodations you reserved were unavailable. Did you ever ask for compensation? Probably not.

As a student, how many times did you accept a grade you didn't deserve because you didn't want to cause a stir by questioning it? Have you ever signed an agreement you hadn't fully read or paid a bill you had a question about just to be polite? Most of us, after years of being conditioned to do so, accept the status quo. We do what we are told and take as gospel statements made by people who have no business or authority to make them.

Being a successful negotiator means you've got to question the signs around you. It means not automatically accepting the status quo because it's the policy. Being a successful negotiator means always being willing to ask for more or better when you're entitled to it—*or even if you're not!*

If you have ever said, "I couldn't possibly ask—they'll just say no," decide right now that you have said those words for the last time! Remember: *Everything* is negotiable. Just as the flipped coin won't always come up heads (or tails), the party on the other side of your negotiation won't *always* say no. Then again, they'll never say yes if you don't ask!

The Five Secrets of Successful Negotiators

The points described in this section aren't secret in the sense that you'll be hearing from my legal team if you reveal them, but secret in the sense that they just don't occur to most people. Here are five important pieces of information without which truly successful negotiation is impossible.

Secret #1: Get Around the Rules

From the beginning, we are all taught to obey the rules. For most of us it starts in school and pretty much never ends. Remember? "Color inside the lines!" "Raise your hand before you speak!" "Get a gold star if you obey the rules; get a demerit if you don't."

Maybe these rules made for an orderly classroom, but they also seem to have set up a conditioning process by which we tend to accept rules without question—even when they don't make much sense. The beat goes on in adult life with such gems as "Don't Even Think of Parking Here!" "Do Not Enter!" "Payment Must Be Received by . . . ," and "Do Not Remove This Tag under Penalty of Law." There are enough conditions on the back of any airline ticket to make you wish you took the bus. Even rental videos and DVDs start out with a needlessly ominous FBI warning!

By adulthood, we are such compliant souls that we often sign agreements that contain rules to which no one in their right mind (if they bothered to read the microscopic print) would agree. One of my favorites is on the back of various retail and credit agreements. It says some version of the following: "In the event of a dispute, you the customer agrees to pay all reasonable legal and court fees incurred in the settlement of that dispute." Translation: "If we disagree, I hereby treat you, the vendor, to a free lawsuit!" When I question such nonsense, I often hear, "Nobody ever questioned that before." That's *always* a good sign.

As if all these rules weren't enough of an outrage, they are often enforced by an army of bureaucrats whose chief function is the utterance of such lines as "It's the policy" or "It's procedure."

Bonus Tip

Don't try to reason with these functionaries. Go over their heads.

Against this formidable backdrop I am telling you that to be a successful negotiator, you have to break the rules. No, I don't mean rip down a "No Parking" sign in your neighborhood. I am telling you to question any odd or unfair policy. Just because there is a rule doesn't mean you can't be exempted from it. Remember: Anytime you hear the words "No one has ever questioned this policy before," you are well on your way to being a successful negotiator.

Secret #2: Go Straight to the Top

The most skilled negotiator won't get anywhere if he or she is talking to the wrong person—a person with no authority to make changes in the status quo. If the individual you're talking to is (1) behind a window,

(2) wearing a name tag, or (3) has a title that begins with the word "assistant," you're talking to the wrong person. You need to get to the real decision maker rather than someone whose job it is to keep you from talking to the right person.

Most of the people you will meet at the cash register, at the front desk, or even in the complaint department are likely to be earning just above minimum wage for a position with below-minimum authority. The give-and-take that is required in any kind of negotiation is impossible in the sea of rules in which these functionaries swim. This situation is rampant from retailers to phone companies to banks to chain operations of all sorts.

No matter how politely you ask if there is someone else you can talk to, your question is still likely to come off as something akin to "You're not worth talking to. Is there someone else around here who can get things done?" Either you get a curt "No, I'm the only one here," or the employee you're speaking to retreats to the back room and, in briefing his or her higher-up on the situation, translates your request into "I hate to bother you, but there's some jerk out there who won't take no for an answer!" That's hardly a good posture from which to begin negotiating.

Here is how I make sure I get to talk to the decision maker: If I'm in the furniture section of a department store and I want to talk to someone beyond the floor personnel—someone who can get things done—I'll go to another part of the store (or come back during another shift, if it's a small place) and say something like, "I've gotten such great service from the furniture department, I wanted to write a letter and maybe get certain people a raise or promotion. Whom should I contact?" In response to that question, most functionaries will give you all but the CEO's cell phone number . . . and sometimes even more.

Bonus Tip #1
Be sure to ask for additional names once you succeed in getting someone to "sing."

> **Bonus Tip #2**
>
> *You may want to ask more than one person just to make sure you're getting the correct name(s). Armed with this information, you can go back to your original target and ask to speak with Mr./Ms. Big, as if you and the boss have lunch twice a week. Your target is likely to be so thrown by the fact that you knew that name, you may even get results right there on the spot. The difference is that you are now operating in a position of power and authority instead of being viewed as "that jerk who won't take no for an answer."*

Secret #3: Don't Get Angry; Get Action

Once you meet with the decision maker, you improve your chances of success by being a person with whom it is pleasant to negotiate. If you have a legitimate complaint, being confrontational (as in loud) or obnoxious (as in spewing demands) makes the issue your behavior instead of the matter you want to negotiate. You won't have much of a chance of getting what you want if the decision maker has to manage two problems—your behavior *and* the negotiation—instead of one.

Obnoxious people also arouse the I'm-not-going-to-take-that-from-him [or her] mentality, which, at the end of the day, is going to get you less than if you had presented the problem firmly and politely to the decision maker. If negotiation fails, there may be a need to become confrontational, but keep that as an option rather than an initial method of approach.

Secret #4: Never Negotiate in a Crowd

In a formal negotiation setting (See Chapter 5) where both the gathering and the issues are large, crowds may be unavoidable, but informal negotiations (one-on-one with minor issues) should be a private affair. Successful negotiation means that someone is going to make a concession—something no one likes to do publicly. If you're going to try to get a better price on a purchase—be it in a store, a flea market, or an auto showroom—do it in private. If anyone but you and your target can hear the conversation, don't even think of negotiating. If other customers hear what's going on, they'll want the same deal. If another salesperson is around, you might fall prey to a pair of salespersons playing a game of "nail the customer" in which *you* are the prize.

You already know enough not to ask for a raise in a crowded elevator. No employer is going to say yes if doing so is going to create an avalanche of "me too" requests. As a negotiator, you can't get what you want in any of these situations unless you do it privately. Talk to the boss, the merchant, or whomever you negotiate with in private, and, whenever possible, do it on a one-on-one basis. Having more than one party present gives the appearance of "ganging up" on the target, and needlessly increases the pressure felt by your fellow negotiator.

Secret #5: Give in Order to Get

A common misconception about negotiators is that success means walking away with all but their target's shirt, leaving that only out of pity for their hapless prey. The truth is that effective negotiators give in order to get. The trick, however, is to give away something that's of little or no value to you but of some real or imagined value to your target.

For example, if I want a better price on an airline ticket or a service upgrade, I'll often begin with something like "I know you didn't come up with this price yourself, and I'm sorry to bother you with it, but if you'd take a look at . . ." After hours of facing the I'll-never-fly-your-crummy-airline-again crowd, that bit of recognition and respect (which costs me nothing) has gotten me a lot of upgrades. In this instance, I gave up an intangible (recognition) and received a tangible benefit in exchange.

At other times, you may need to give a tangible item to gain a benefit. In those cases, take a close inventory of what you have to give in order to find a tangible that the other side will value, but that you can easily do without. As a customer, you might consider swapping an extended warranty for a lower price, particularly if you intend to replace the purchase before that warranty expires. As a vendor, you might offer extra service or an exclusive hotline number for that customer. (At least you can tell them it's exclusive).

Vendors are great at coming up with giveaways that seem substantial to customers but are of little or no cost to the vendors themselves. For example, automobile dealers lure customers with promises for "free oil changes for as long as you own your car!" At first glance, that sounds like a great deal. But think about it: If you keep the car for five years and have maybe ten oil changes, that perk will cost the dealer less than $150. That's very little comparatively if the dealership makes $2,000 profit on the car and even less if the dealer adds the cost of the oil changes to the selling price (and don't think they won't).

While negotiating, think about what you want, but also think about what you can give up in exchange. Whenever possible, it should be an intangible or a tangible of minimal cost, yet the recipient should perceive it as valuable. However, it may also mean giving up a part of your initial position in order to reach the ultimate goal of all negotiation: agreement.

Summary

Negotiation is both a science and an art—the science being the strategies you employ and the art being the knowledge of when and to whom to apply them as you work your way toward agreement. But before becoming a successful negotiator, you will also need to peel away the layers of conditioning that cause you to conform without questioning the status quo. Especially as you start out on your journey toward becoming a master negotiator, it is essential to be willing to negotiate when you are less than comfortable doing so. Dispelling that discomfort you might feel is just the beginning of breaking down the barriers that discourage you from negotiating and gaining the advantage you seek and, in all likelihood, deserve!

Key Thoughts and Takeaway Points

Negotiation is not just a process; it's an attitude. This attitude is defined by the notion that anytime there is an advantage to be gained from talking about an issue, you should negotiate your way to that advantage.

Negotiation is *not* confrontation. Confrontation is a one-time, win-or-lose situation that typically ends with such words as "Take it or leave it!" Confrontation should be reserved for when you are willing and able to walk away if the outcome is not in your favor.

***Everything* is negotiable!** The successful negotiator has internalized and, in a communicative sense, lives by that motto—a state of mind that will make the sea of signs, instructions, and rules that surrounds you seem more like highly negotiable suggestions!

CHAPTER TWO

Guerrilla Negotiation Tactics

AT-A-GLANCE SUMMARY
This chapter gives you the tools you need to get started negotiating: a series of easily applied verbal tactics designed to give you the advantage in situations where you should negotiate but haven't done so in the past. You'll also learn how to resist pressure tactics designed to discourage your negotiation efforts.

Making the First Moves

Reading about techniques and strategies may be part of the picture, but relying solely on the printed word to become an adept negotiator is like learning to swim by phone. You won't get anywhere unless you dive into the pool, and the sooner you take the plunge, the better. Building negotiation skills works the same way. You have got to begin applying negotiation tactics to real-life situations in order to develop and build your negotiation skills. That's what this chapter is about: giving you the tools you need to get started.

This chapter presents a series of "guerrilla negotiation tactics" that you can begin to use right away. What follows is a series of negotiation tactics that, with practice, you can use with devastating effect to gain the advantage you seek.

Guerrilla Negotiation Tactics

Guerrilla Tactic #1: The Basic Ultimatum

Not to be confused with a threat, an ultimatum is simply a statement of your objection to a situation or condition followed by a strategic silence. Suppose you're checking into a hotel, and through someone's error, the type of room you reserved is unavailable. Don't get angry—negotiate!

WHAT TO SAY: Start with something like "I reserved a suite, a single room is completely unacceptable!" followed by a deliberate silence.

WHEN TO SAY IT: Use an ultimatum anytime you get less than you wanted or less than you deserve, be it the faulty or incomplete car repair, the meal that's not to your liking, poorly done dry cleaning, and so on. Once you get a positive response, politely press for more. If they offer you a discount, ask for a larger one or a free night's stay. Of course they'll fix the car, but have them double the usual warranty for that repair. Once they give up something, they have demonstrated their willingness to negotiate. That's your cue to try to get even more!

WARNINGS: Always deliver the ultimatum calmly so that your behavior isn't cause for comment. This keeps your target focused on the issue, not you. Also, don't turn the ultimatum into a threat: "If you don't do something about this, you'll hear from my lawyers!" (Do you really think your lawyer would get involved in this?) or "I'll never eat here again!" (Are you really someone they want to see again?) Be polite and firm, and, once you get the initial concession, go for more. I wouldn't leave the hotel front desk without a huge discount or a coupon for a free future stay. Neither should you.

Bonus Tip

As in any negotiation, as you deliver the ultimatum, maintain eye contact with your target. An averted or darting glance will be perceived as weakness and a lack of belief in your position.

Guerrilla Tactic #2: The Ultimatum Plus

A variation on the first tactic, the Ultimatum Plus consists of the "unacceptability" statement plus a specific demand.

WHAT TO SAY: "These accommodations are unacceptable and I'll do with nothing less than an upgrade to the concierge floor." In this case, you have decided exactly what you want from the situation and are adding a demand to the statement of unacceptability.

WHEN TO SAY IT: Use this tactic anytime you receive subpar service and have a specific outcome or objective in mind, for example, a full refund, a future discount, or any reasonable concession you can expect to gain.

WARNING: The key to success here is keeping your demand reasonable and maintaining your willingness to accept a counteroffer. The fact is that once they offer you anything, you've succeeded and are playing with house money. Be wary, though, of demands that are completely unreasonable, for example, "If you can't come up with a nonsmoking room, I demand nothing less than a one-week stay at one of your resort properties." With this demand, you have just crossed the line from negotiation to confrontation, and now your target has to win by saying no instead of agreeing with a reasonable position and granting a concession.

Guerrilla Tactic #3: The Ultimatum Exit

The strongest ultimatum, this tactic is reserved for those times when you want something big. For example, when you discover that a contractor has no intention of beginning work on the date initially agreed upon, either you want action, or you want to get out.

WHAT TO SAY: "These starting and completion dates just won't do. Either you show up on the date in the contract or I'm hiring another firm. It's your choice, but if you make the wrong one, you can forget about my future business as well."

WHEN TO SAY IT: The priority here is to get the problem solved. If it won't be solved this way, you may need to go elsewhere. Before making the decision to employ the Ultimatum Exit tactic, make sure you have somewhere else to go. Once again, don't get loud; be firm but polite.

This is negotiation with a strong dose of confrontation, but there may be no alternative.

WARNING: The confrontational nature of the Ultimatum Exit tactic is not to be confused with bluffing. *Always* have an alternative when you use this strategy. If you have to come crawling back because you really didn't have somewhere else to go, you'll do so at a permanent disadvantage.

Guerrilla Tactic #4: Research and Destroy

Information is power, and this tactic is an example of using that power to get what you want. Successful application of the Research and Destroy tactic is simply a matter of getting your information in order and presenting the target with the folly of his or her position. For example, anytime a competitor has a lower price, use that information in order to "destroy" the target's position.

WHAT TO SAY: "We both know Axle Motors is selling this same vehicle for $850 less. If you want this sale, you're going to have to beat their price." (*Note:* Matching a competitor's price is assumed. The request [or demand] is to *do better*. Otherwise, you're not really negotiating, but asking for something you can already get elsewhere.)

WHEN TO SAY IT: Use this tactic anytime there is something wrong with a deal and you can come up with the facts to prove it; for example, the merchandise is not the same as that in the ad; the price isn't competitive; the finance rate is too high. Whatever the situation, having the facts is essential in getting what you want.

CAUTION: Telling someone he or she is wrong can be seen as confrontational, which makes some people defensive to the point of irrationality. If you've caught the target in a lie, the volume of their expression of outrage will most often be proportionate to the degree of their dishonesty. Be prepared to walk in this situation. If something is that wrong with a deal or a price, you really shouldn't be doing business with these people.

Bonus Tip

The Internet has put massive amounts of information at your fingertips—everything from little-known product discontinuations to hidden incentives and discounts, to name just a few. Use it to your advantage.

Guerrilla Tactic #5: Goodwill Hunting

This tactic is about hunting for an advantage and using goodwill as your weapon. Service personnel and customer-contact representatives all endure hours of training on how to handle tough customers and difficult people. The other side of that coin is that they have *no* training on how to handle nice people. That lack of training presents an opportunity—a chance to appeal to their goodwill!

WHAT TO SAY: In dealing with customer-contact personnel, pay a compliment ("Does that tag say you've been working here for ten years? That's an impressive record!") or get them talking about themselves ("Many more hours before you get to go home?"). Follow that conversation with a mild-mannered inquiry as to whether you can get a better price, longer warranty, or the like, or if anyone there can authorize the advantage you want. The point here is to trade a bit of goodwill for some kind of advantage or concession.

WHEN TO SAY IT: Use this tactic at airline counters, rental car companies, or retail stores, where salespeople work on commission and have some discretionary power. In short, this tactic is worth trying on any customer-contact person who has to deal with difficult people all day. By simply being the opposite, you are likely to gain an advantage.

CAUTION: This is a soft-sell form of negotiation based on having established goodwill. If it fails, there's no need to be dejected or withdraw your compliments. The strongest method you should employ in this situation is to inquire whether there is anyone present who could get you that concession.

Bonus Tip

Whenever possible, get in line behind a belligerent customer. The employee who has just been put through some abuse and perhaps has given some in return will be grateful to meet up with any expression of goodwill and is likely to respond favorably to your requests.

Guerrilla Tactic #6: Solve a Problem

This tactic is about presenting what you want out of a negotiation as a solution to a problem, rather than something your target is giving up. It works well toward the end of a sale if there is still a lot of inventory around or when you are close to earning a frequent flyer award and the airline rep is given "an opportunity" to dispose of the airline's debt to you.

WHAT TO SAY: "We both know the sale is about over and you still have quite a bit of this outdoor furniture left. How much more of a break can I get if I double my initial order?"

You're getting more, and at a larger discount, but—most important—you've simultaneously solved the merchant's problem. ("I'll reduce your inventory even more, in exchange for a break.") This way you both gain—or at least you're presenting it that way.

WHEN TO SAY IT: When making off-season purchases, when buying late in clearance sales, or anytime a vendor is dealing with a piece of merchandise that doesn't fly off the shelves, solve the target's problem by taking it off his or her hands—but only at a reduced price!

CAUTION: Be gracious in "solving the problem." Nobody likes getting kicked when they're down, nor does anyone like the person who does it. Seeming triumphant or in anyway gleeful about your target's plight is a mistake. Doing so may throw the target into a state of denial and cause him or her to wait for a better day rather than give you an advantage.

Guerrilla Tactic #7: The Cash Flash

A version of the Cash Flash was often seen on the old TV game show *Let's Make a Deal*. The premise was that a contestant could select a prize hidden behind one of three doors. There was one valuable prize (a cruise or even a car), but the other two doors concealed such treasures as heads of cabbage or bales of hay. Just as the contestant made a selection, the host would heighten the suspense by pulling out a roll of bills and saying, "I'll give you ten of these one-hundred-dollar bills right now, *or* you can choose to look behind the curtain you've chosen." Sometimes contestants took the cash; sometimes they won a big prize. At other times, they went home with a few bales of hay. The program may not have been a cultural high spot, but it taught us volumes about how people react to the sight of money. The stuff has an amazing ability to cloud logic.

WHAT TO SAY: "I'm interested, and I've got six hundred dollars cash with me . . ." I've used the Cash Flash on several occasions with amazing results. Here's how it works: Determine the asking price in advance; then stuff 60 percent (or less) of that figure in large-denomination bills into your pocket. After examining the item, using lots of strategic silence to heighten the vendor's tension level, take the money out of your pocket and say "How about five hundred dollars—cash—right now?"

WHEN TO SAY IT: Use this tactic in any substantial transaction where cash is an option. More often than not, the Cash Flash produces a bit of grumbling about the low offer and how the target really wanted more, but the sight of the cash works its magic and you end up with a bargain. Since merchants have to fork over a percentage of each credit card sale to the card company, they are often willing to provide a discount if you give them cash. However, beware; make this concession only on low-risk items because once you buy it, you own it!

Getting the Lowest Price

When most people negotiate, it's usually about price and how to get the merchant, the contractor, the homeowner, or whomever the vendor is to drop the price. The simple key to getting the best price is being direct enough to ask for *exactly* what you want. Instead, most people simply ask for a price and then walk away in silence once it doesn't meet their expectations or requirements. If this scenario is repeated often enough, eventually one lucky person will receive the cumulative benefit of all those failed transactions as the merchant capitulates. Instead, simply ask for the better price. Don't blurt out an offer; let your target name the first number. (It might be lower than your intended initial offering, so you gain nothing by being the first to talk numbers.) In this way you will seize the cumulative benefit of those nonnegotiators who simply walked away. When you're talking price, there are also a couple of principles you should bear in mind:

Behind Every Huge Discount, There's an Equally Huge Lie!

Think of the fabulous deals and big discounts you've sought, only to find a bucket of mud at the end of the rainbow: Take the car dealer who promises $1,500 for any trade-in, no matter what the condition. The dealer can give you this trade-in value for any wreck you push into the place because he or she is already charging $1,500 too much for the car you're about to purchase. Or consider the chain store that has a going-out-of-business sale announcing 50 to 70 percent savings on all remaining merchandise. Of course, what the store is not saying is that it's sold off all the decent goods to a competitor and the stuff on sale will end up in a Dumpster if you don't buy it.

Even though we're talking here about getting the best price, if the seller immediately knocks 50 percent *or more* off a price, unless you're at a fire sale, be careful. Check things out before you commit. I'd like to think you got that tremendous break because after reading only this far, you've become a fabulous negotiator, but even if you are, outlandish discounts should arouse your suspicions.

There Will Never Be Another Opportunity Like This!

This is not a negotiating principle but a pressure tactic that should send you running! This line is true if you're buying the Brooklyn Bridge, but if you believe it, I probably could sell you the Brooklyn Bridge. It's used to create a false sense of urgency and is true only in the rarest of circumstances. Anytime you're being urged to "act now!" my reaction is, "If I don't act now, they'll have a tough time coming up with another sucker."

The pressure to "act now" is sometimes couched in popular myths. In real estate, the maxim "Buy land; they're not making any more of it" sounds pretty bulletproof until you stop and think that people move away, they die, and the real estate industry has yet to run out of inventory. Another favorite of mine is "Prices have never been lower!" That's true, and you'd better buy now—unless you want to wait until prices drop further!

For me the ultimate destroyer of the myth that there will never be another deal like this is the line I see in newspapers on a very regular basis. At the top of the ad in bold letters it says, "Repeat of a Sellout!" If you believe the folks who say things like this, meet me in Brooklyn. I've got this bridge I'd like you to look at! Price negotiation, especially when you can go elsewhere, should approach confrontation; that is, you're willing to win or walk away. If you're willing to walk away and mean it, you've got the upper hand.

Summary

With review and repetition, these guerrilla negotiation tactics *can* and *should* become part of your arsenal of precise and strategic tactics rather than random behaviors when you're faced with a situation where you *can* or *should* have the advantage. These tactics, along with a greater willingness to negotiate, will bring you results in situations where most people just walk away, either because they are unwilling to negotiate or because they just never thought it would work. As one imbued with the negotiator's attitude, you may not *always* achieve the result you expected, but you'll always be leagues ahead of the vast majority of people who never even try.

Key Thoughts and Takeaway Points

How do you get to Carnegie Hall? In this ancient joke, a tourist asks this question of a New York cop. The officer's response? "Practice!" The same is true of building your proficiency as a negotiator—practice!

Surprise yourself and negotiate! The reason you are reading this book is that you're not used to negotiation as an internalized behavior. Practice is essential in helping you to develop your own negotiation mentality rather than viewing the art and science of negotiation as an abstract, as most people do.

Look at the numbers with a sharp and skeptical eye. When talking about prices and numbers in negotiation, beware of numbers that are too far from reality, or rapid and unprovoked price collapses. As I point out in this chapter, behind every huge discount there is often an equally huge lie. Be vigilant in the presence of rapidly changing numbers!

CHAPTER THREE

Basic Training for Negotiators

AT-A-GLANCE SUMMARY
This chapter is about giving you the experience you need to develop an improved level of comfort as a negotiator. It includes a series of real-life scenarios in which you can negotiate, as well as guidance on which tactics work best. Bonus tips and cautions are also part of this chapter's mission of helping you to build the confidence you need to succeed at negotiation.

Gaining Hands-on Experience

To begin your basic negotiation training, I have chosen a series of situations in which we all find ourselves but in which we don't usually negotiate. Success in any or all of these moments is good practice for more crucial situations. There are three major objectives to keep in mind as you go through basic training: (1) the realization that you *can* and *should* negotiate more than you do; (2) the knowledge that every negotiation is unique, and the results, while often positive, are always unpredictable; and (3) the establishment of a greater comfort level as you gain experience. In addition, as you apply the guerrilla tactics from Chapter 2, you'll begin to discover which tactics are best suited to your interpersonal style.

As you begin to develop your negotiation skills, the right perspective is important. While it's true that everything is negotiable, it doesn't mean that everything is *worth* negotiating. While I would encourage you to negotiate more than you have in the past, don't transform yourself into the neighborhood pariah, fighting with the guy at the produce stand over the price of lettuce.

The scenarios that follow are a good starting point in that they are real-life situations in which you should be able to gain an advantage. However, they are noncrucial; that is, if you don't attain the desired outcome, life as you know it will go on and you will have learned something about negotiation—what works and what doesn't work. Also, don't forget that each negotiation is unique. You may do an excellent job hitting all the strategic notes you intended. However, your target may actually be reacting to something that happened earlier in the day—taking out his or her frustration with someone else on you. The result: a failed outing despite your best efforts. Alternatively, there will be times when everything works and you achieve results beyond your expectations.

Keep trying! If you fail dismally at one attempt, you'll get to practice before a completely different set of people next time using the lessons learned from your prior efforts. After a few ventures, given your increased comfort level and self-knowledge, you'll find that your ability to get results will improve exponentially. The important thing is to *get into the game and keep playing!*

Here, then, is a series of noncrucial but real-life scenarios in which you can and should seek the advantage. Let's negotiate!

The Location of the Restaurant Table

When you enter a restaurant, there are all sorts of reasons why you get seated where you do, from balancing the workload of the staff to which "regulars" are coming in later for their favorite table. Notice that neither of these reasons has anything to do with *your* comfort or pleasure. Inevitably someone is going to be seated at the traffic-laden sites nearest the entrance or the table that is barely missed by the kitchen door as it flies open every twenty-four seconds. Of course, there are also those tables in the far-flung corners of the dining room where shipping your meal via Federal Express would seem an option.

GOAL: A better location.

TACTIC: **Ultimatum Plus.** "This table is unacceptable. What about that one?" A bit softer: "We'd like a quieter table" followed by a silence.

The Credit Card Interest Rate

If you're in the mood to be shocked, take a look at the interest rate charged by the typical credit card company, which, at the time of this writing, often exceeds 20 percent. Balance that against the fact that you, every member of your family, and perhaps even your dog are being bombarded with ads inviting you to sign up for yet another swim with these sharks. The competition is fierce, and that gives you an advantage. These people want your business and are often willing to reduce their rate of interest just to keep you as a customer. *All you have to do is ask!*

GOAL: A lower rate.

TACTIC: **Research and Destroy.** Suggested telephone conversation: "Hello. My name is Pat. What's your name?" (The copious use of first names—and, of course, you should use your own—warms the tone of the conversation so it can be questioning without being confrontational.) "Bill, I've been a loyal cardholder for a long time. I just got an ad from your competitor [give the name of said competitor], and frankly I'm shocked. Their interest rate is thirty percent less than yours." (Tell the truth; don't give just the teaser rate. These people may be shady, but they're not ill informed.) "If I can't get a lower rate, I'm going to have to cancel and sign up with a competitor. How much can you lower my rate?" You should get results. If you don't, call back again or ask to speak with a supervisor. If you can't get anywhere, it might be time to switch!

The Hotel Room

Just slightly less complex than the U.S. tax code is the logic by which hotels set their rates. As the seasoned traveler may know, there are corporate rates, special corporate rates, convention rates, government rates, group rates, and many others as well.

GOAL: A better room, a lower rate . . . maybe both!

Tactic: **Goodwill Hunting / Solve a Problem.** "It's been a long day for both of us, but I have to ask. This rate is higher than the one I was quoted. I know you didn't make the quote, but could you look into it? I'd like a better room [larger room, higher floor, concierge level, free breakfast]." You've established goodwill ("It's been a long day for both of us . . .") and just about said you don't want to argue—but there is this problem that you hope the target can solve. You may have to politely go to a supervisor, but try to get something through the negotiation with first person you speak to.

The Department Store

The secret weapon that has greatly discouraged us as negotiators is the price tag. Most of us seem transfixed by it and wouldn't think of questioning it. It's strange. After all, if you get an unfair parking ticket, you question it. If you get an inaccurate bill in the mail, you question it and get an adjustment. But most of us bow in obedience to the tiny price tag.

Goal: A price reduction.

Tactic: **Solve a Problem / Goodwill Hunting.** The approach: "It will be going on sale shortly; how much better can you do on this? Can the manager get me a discount?" I have often negotiated successfully in department stores although I usually—politely—have to negotiate with a person one level up from the floor salesperson.

Frequent Flier Miles

They've been called the S&H green stamps of the new millennium, and stories abound of those who have flown around the world and vacationed for free with the mileage they earned doing everything from buying dessert topping to making mortgage payments. Your advantage here is that airlines have to carry these miles as a kind of debt, so even if you're a bit short of miles for a particular perk, try to get it anyhow. In fact, if you don't get results, keep calling; some agents are more flexible than others.

GOAL: Getting more for less.

TACTIC: **Solve a Problem.** "Hi my name is Pat. What's yours? Alice, I am trying to book a vacation for two, and I'm just short of mileage for the two tickets. I've been a loyal customer for years and I was hoping that would get me some consideration in the form of a break." Follow this statement with a strategic silence. If you need more ammunition: "Getting these miles off your books is good for the airline. It would solve a problem for both of us. Alice, maybe you could speak to someone there—I'd appreciate it." Note that what you are doing is giving the target an advantage or referring to the problem of the miles on the airline's books. Also, note the use of names to make the negotiation more personal and friendly. If you don't get results, call back and try again!

Off-Season / End of Season

Stores that have clearance sales are in essence saying, "Look, we screwed up, and we're going to let this stuff go cheap rather than keep it for another year." Keep in mind that you're at an advantage here, since it costs money to ship merchandise back to a warehouse, store it all year, and then ship it back to the showroom again. Not only do they want to get rid of merchandise, it's also in their best interest.

GOAL: An *even bigger* discount.

TACTIC: **Ultimatum / Exit and Solve a Problem.** "Markdown or not, these prices still seem high. A bigger discount will benefit both of us. . . . How much better can you do? Who can get me a better deal?" Your approach should be polite, logical, persistent, and ready to make an exit. (Of course, you'll be back again during the next shift.)

A Quantity Discount

A universal business rule is that the more you buy, the less you pay. Whenever possible, you should be sure this applies to you. Admittedly, you're never going to buy as many Fords as Hertz, but as I hope you've already learned, you should always ask for a discount.

GOAL: A better price. However, don't begin with a quantity discount. Get the very best price you can on a single item, using one or a selection of strategies.

TACTIC: **Ultimatum Plus.** After you're certain you've got the best price, pose a simple question: "How much for two?" Follow this with an additional request: "Suppose I take a dozen?"

Bonus Tip

By beginning with a negotiation for a discount on one, and then getting a discount for two, you establish that the quantity discount is in effect. If you get the discount for two, logic dictates that the more you buy, the better you'll do, only because you established the cycle.

CAUTION: This tactic may have limited effectiveness when prices are really at rock bottom.

Damaged Goods

If you've owned enough products made by humans, you may have noticed that imperfections abound. They are often minor and don't affect the functioning of the item, or the imperfection may be obvious but of no consequence to you. For example, I once got an incredible deal on a sofa that had a slight tear on one end, an end that would always be against a wall in my apartment and therefore never visible to anyone. If the flaw is of no consequence to you (which you should never admit), you may have a great opportunity for a real bargain!

GOAL: A discount on a sub-par purchase.

TACTIC: **Solve a problem.** "I really like that piece of furniture over there [make the salesperson think you're hooked], but it's damaged. How much of a break can I get if I take it off your hands?" No luck? Ask for a supervisor or whoever can make a decision, and begin again.

Bonus Tip #1

Stores, especially large ones, may have policies about not selling damaged items. You'll have to talk your way around these policies. I once had a store manager admit that an item would be shipped back to a clearance center, stored, and eventually marked down and sold at a discount. I offered to merely take the discount right then and save the cost of all that shipping and handling. After quite a bit of talking, I got the item at nearly 50 percent off the list price.

Bonus Tip #2

I have found that negotiating in places where staff members don't usually negotiate is best accomplished at odd hours, such as before closing time, when staffers are tired and senior management isn't around to crack the whip. Near closing time, you also are more likely to be dealing with a part-time employee, who is less likely to let company loyalty get in the way of your gaining an advantage.

Asking for a Raise

This is not really a negotiation scenario but a communicative encounter that provokes high levels of tension in those who attempt it because of the success/failure nature of the mission. You'll note that I have included asking for a raise in a section of noncrucial scenarios. I have done so because even if you fail, this quest informs those you are asking that you'd like *more*, and presents the possibility of some delayed results. It is also noncrucial in that failure to gain your objective doesn't preclude your trying again later.

GOAL: A salary bump.

TACTIC: **The Ultimatum.** By using the ultimatum in this situation, I don't mean begin by saying "If I don't get a raise, I'm walking, dammit." But you should begin by saying just what you want, as in, "Ed, I'd like to have an increase in pay." Note that I started with a name, a certain way to capture the attention of your target. The typical seeker of increased compensation begins his or her request with a statement such as "You know I've been with the company a long time, and I feel greatly responsible for much of the success we've enjoyed, and so I was thinking it might be a good time to ask . . ."

What you are doing with this type of request is presenting a defense when none is required. Also, by not getting to the question quickly enough, you telegraph where you are going and with this ramble give any manager time to assemble a negative response. Finally, by putting your request at the end of your statement instead of the very beginning, you are signaling your own discomfort. This discomfort will be seen as self-doubt, which translates into a reason for the manager to refuse your request.

In asking for a raise, use the name of the person to whom you're talking, and put the request in the very first phrase you utter. You can include your justification in the conversation that follows, where, especially if you've already made your request, it will not be perceived as defensive. Once again, this may not be a negotiation scenario in the strict sense. However, the confidence you gain from even making the effort will be a powerful tool in other negotiation-oriented encounters.

The Mini-Injustice

I am probably telling you something you already know when I say that life is unfair. As a negotiation exercise, take one of the mini-injustices in your life and see if you can change it. Here is a mini-injustice I experienced recently:

I had the misfortune of having to pick up someone on a Sunday night at a major airport. As is true at many major airports, crowds and security concerns preclude meeting a passenger at a terminal. Typically, you have to drive to a parking lot, walk to the terminal, find your guest, and then walk back to your car. Of course, you have to pay to park, even if only for a few minutes. The mini-injustice occurred as I tried to leave the parking lot. As I was leaving, so were about three hundred other people, resulting in a forty-minute backup as each motorist dutifully coughed up the parking fee.

Upon reaching the gate, instead of paying, I asked to see a supervisor (don't talk to clerks) and politely explained that I would pay to park but not to wait on line for forty minutes. The result? I paid only to park—not to wait on line.

GOAL: Circumvent an unfair situation.

TACTIC: **The Ultimatum.** "I'm willing to pay to park, but not to wait on line."

While the amount of money (a few dollars) may have been trivial, the experience wasn't. In that simple negotiation, I questioned authority, got to the right person, and through *politely* taking a position that seemed firm, I gained fair treatment. By the way, I was only playing a negotiating game, and I was bluffing. Had the manager been insistent, I had the remaining money in hand and was ready to give in. But he didn't know that, and I not only prevailed but got in a quick practice session and righted a mini-injustice.

Summary

Each of these situations is noncrucial; that is, if you prevail, you'll gain an advantage. If you lose, you'll at least gain an opportunity to examine what you could have done better. In these early attempts, you will probably gain some advantages, and you won't lose a job, a friend, or any cash. You should also note that these are discrete situations; your performance in one won't affect your performance in another. And since none of these people talk one another, they won't realize what you're up to—beginning to think like a negotiator who is *always* willing to negotiate.

In addition to applying these tactics, compile *your own* set of real-life situations comparable to those you have just read about. Use your own scenarios to further develop your negotiation skills. In doing so, you'll be better equipped to negotiate effectively in more serious or even crucial situations.

Key Thoughts and Takeaway Points

Becoming a successful negotiator means finding out what works for *you*. I pointed out earlier that the highly touted and much-cited case-study approach to negotiation holds little validity for me, unless you can guarantee that the same people will be present and all sides of the issue will be presented in *exactly* the same way in each negotiation. It just doesn't happen. The monstrous variable of human interaction will always be there to intervene.

You can manage that variable for yourself by seeing which tactic works in which situation—what works best, or doesn't work, for you as you sharpen your negotiation skills.

Experiment and remember: One adverse outcome does not mean the stage is set for another. As you learn from some of the mistakes you make along the way, remember that each of these negotiations is a *discrete* event and that every new situation is just that—a new beginning and a new opportunity to build your negotiation skills.

PART TWO

Management Skills for Negotiators

CHAPTER FOUR

People Management in Negotiations

AT-A-GLANCE SUMMARY
This chapter is about managing the cast of characters faced by every negotiator at one time or another. Tactics are one part of the equation, but people-management skills are another essential element in gaining the results you want as you negotiate. From tough customers to Bullies and Smiling Cobras, this chapter shows you how to remain in command and negotiate your way to a successful outcome.

Handling Difficult People

Earlier, I pointed out that there are no magic-bullet words in negotiation—phrases that you can simply utter to gain the objective or advantage you are seeking. The reason is that people react differently depending on such variables as how they feel about you, the issue under negotiation, and the personality complex they bring to the negotiation.

There are, however, distinct behaviors that people exhibit in negotiation or in any communicative encounter. Being on the lookout for these behaviors can help you manage the behaviors to your advantage, or even tell you when you should walk away. Here are some of the personality types I've observed in negotiation and some strategies for managing their behavior.

The Martian

The Martian is my term for people who ignore or dismiss factual information, causing you to ask, "What planet are you from?" For example, I was once negotiating a budget figure with a colleague. I wanted the number higher; he wanted it lower. I spent the better part of ten minutes defining *exactly* how my figure was calculated and therefore valid. As I arrived at the last line in the equation, my listener simply shook his head and said, "That means nothing!"

Some negotiators are Martians in that they consistently ignore the facts. In sales they are the people who lose time after time and blame the customer or the product. In any situation, they are the people who just don't get it.

If this person is permanently set on the Martian frequency, there is no point in trying to negotiate. Just in case, give your side between one and three attempts at breaking through and gaining some agreement. For example, with my aforementioned colleague, I'd try one or two more repetitions of my explanation, beginning, "Let me go over those numbers again—I'm sure you'll feel differently." If your explanation continues to fall on deaf ears, walk away. Otherwise, you run the risk of a long and tedious negotiation that is destined to end in failure. Walk away, and save your time and energy for an Earthling!

The Bully

By now, you've read enough to know the difference between negotiation and confrontation. Negotiators are out to seek agreement, whereas those who confront are out to win or hammer the other side into agreement. Since confusion between negotiation and confrontation is rampant, as you negotiate you are going to run across your share of Bullies—people who figure that by getting loud or even profane, they'll gain the upper hand. Typical bullying tactics begin with the personal attack ("You're nuts to think we'll accept this offer!") followed by the attack on your proposal ("We can get a better offer than this from any bum on the street any day of the week!") or your team ("Every one of you must be idiots to even come in here with an offer like this!").

In the fashion of the Bully, these statements are delivered at a needlessly high decibel level just for effect. The Bully's goal is to get you to lose control—to be caught off guard by either his or her words or decibel level to the extent that you'll be rattled enough to respond emotionally. The Bully's game is to throw you off balance so you'll say things you shouldn't say or make concessions you wouldn't normally make.

Responding to the Bully and getting the results you want require a two-part approach—both verbal and nonverbal. Nonverbally, your response should be quieter than that of the Bully. Never deliver a loud response. To do so says that you are no longer in control. In dealing with the Bully, remember: The one who speaks the loudest loses the advantage. Keep cool, maintain eye contact, and speak in a measured, restrained tone of voice.

A further nonverbal technique is to isolate the Bully by directing your responses to the rest of the team, making eye contact with and even positioning your chair to face other team members.

On the verbal side, you should do what Bullies never count on—shove back! Of course, your shove is strictly verbal, but it should consist of a reprimand for the personal affront, which doesn't mention the offense specifically, but takes exception to it. For example: "Your references to my mental stability or that of my team won't be of any help in getting us to numbers we can agree on. On those numbers, what I can tell you is . . ."

What you have communicated with these tactics is that you won't be rattled by the Bully's bluster. In the absence of any effect, the Bully is very likely to quiet down—unless you respond with your own bullying, which merely sets up a bullying contest in which the only issue to be settled is which of you is the loudest or the most profane.

The Bluffer

The Bluffer, a close cousin of the Bully, doesn't deal in anger or bluster; instead, his or her game is the outrageous proposal—for instance, the very high or very low counterproposal that's delivered matter-of-factly, with the logic "It's so crazy it just might work." The Bluffer gets his or her way only when you're insufficiently prepared or so stunned by his or her bravado that you go along or try to reach a middle ground on the outrageous offer.

The best tactic to take with the Bluffer is the flat refusal. Remember, high-ball or low-ball offers are inherently dishonest. Don't respond angrily or get upset by the Bluffer. Unlike the Bully's tactics, this isn't an attempt to upset you; it's an attempt to see how firm your position is and how well prepared you are on the issues at hand. Only the ill prepared or the uninformed can fall prey to the Bluffer. So, in response to the Bluffer, there is no need for emotionality or outrage. Just say no! If you do it quietly and matter-of-factly, the Bluffer will respect you for it.

The Smiling Cobra

Anytime you are in a negotiation session and you find yourself saying, "This is going to be easy," be careful. You might very well be in the presence of what psychologists refer to as the passive/aggressive personality or, as he or she appears at the negotiation table, the Smiling Cobra. It's the strategy of this character to let things move along to the point at which you see yourself virtually racing toward agreement—and then the Smiling Cobra strikes. Suddenly and without warning, the mood changes and the negotiation grinds to a halt as the Smiling Cobra raises an objection—usually a large one—and sticks by it. Here is how a strike from the Smiling Cobra might sound: "I've been sitting here watching this agreement take shape, and all I can say is, I hope you know what you're doing. I think things are moving much too fast, and we might want to go back and revisit much of what has been said because I am very uncomfortable with the whole session." This can be a devastating blow because although it is delivered politely, it threatens to undermine all of the prior efforts.

If confronted with the Smiling Cobra, the best idea is to charm the snake! While it comes in a different form, the Smiling Cobra's strategy is much the same as that of the Bully—to disrupt in a big way and throw you and your team off balance. The temptation is to attack with a loud "Why did you wait until now? You're just trying to grab power here for your own petty reasons while the rest of us . . ." What you *should* do is get the Smiling Cobra talking about his or her discomfort, for example, "I'm sorry you feel that way. Let's go back if we need to, but tell us specifically what you find problematic. I don't want anyone here to be uncomfortable."

With this type of response, you demonstrate that you're not threatened, his or her discomfort is not something you seek, and you're willing to go back to review the negotiation points. With these words and a willingness to revisit issues, you have just charmed the Cobra!

The Perry Mason

The grandfather of TV courtroom dramas, the show was defined by Attorney Perry Mason's surgically precise cross-examination, which usually resulted in the guilty party (who invariably was in the courtroom) jumping up and bursting into an unexpected "Okay, okay, you've got me!" confession.

Some negotiators play their game with this kind of litigator's zeal, hoping to happen upon that piece of information that will cause your entire case to crumble. Their disagreement is usually on small issues, for example, "On page twenty-three of the contract, the figure of $2,000 should really read $2,023," or "Does the language on page seven mean that delivery will be *by* the seventh of the month or *on* the seventh of the month?"

When dealing with the Perry Mason, it's essential to remember: Give up a checker—but never the game! There is nothing you can say that will neutralize the Perry Mason. Assuming you can prove this character wrong on one item, he or she will simply go to another, and another, and another.

Effective containment of the prosecutor means providing a constant stream of evidence in a conciliatory tone with responses such as "Perry, I appreciate your attention to detail, but I really do have every confidence in our numbers." If you must (i.e., if it will move things along), give up a checker to the Perry Mason. For example: "Perry, which would you prefer: a delivery on the seventh or a delivery by the seventh? Just let me know and I'll arrange it."

When dealing with this character, remember: The Perry Mason is just as much an irritant to his own team as he is to yours. So, express confidence in your own position, give up a minor checker here or there, but at no time try to restrain or neutralize the Perry Mason. If you do, you'll just ignite this character's prosecutorial instincts and make him or her press harder.

The Bozo

Silence in most communicative activities, including negotiation, is often equated with failure, whereas talking is equated with success. Thus, there will come a time in any session when someone (the Bozo) who up to that time hasn't spoken will feel the need to say *something*, no matter how inane, irrelevant, or even destructive it might be. Remarks born out of a need to say something are usually the product of a person who has spent little or no time paying attention to the negotiation. Another version of the Bozo is the late arrival, who tries to compensate with a flurry of participation, no matter how meaningless it might be.

Your top weapons against the Bozo are a smile, an affirmative nod, and a quick review. The Bozo is harmless unless you attempt to take him or her on for lack of participation or late arrival. No matter how justified your negative reaction to the Bozo's participation, resist the temptation. Instead, be supportive of the Bozo. For example, if he or she is talking about the disposal of PCBs and erringly says PVCs (a typical Bozo error), or if he or she begins talking about an issue that was already discussed and agreed upon, let the Bozo know of the error, but do so gently. An appropriately low-key but corrective response should sound like this: "If you're referring to the PCB problem, I believe we reached a settlement on the issue, but maybe you think a review of the matter would be constructive."

With this response, you've corrected the error and restated the facts but given the option for the Bozo to proceed with correct information. Odds are that the Bozo will just go away because he or she never intended to participate, but wanted only to *seem* like an active participant.

The Gadfly

The Gadfly is the member of a negotiating team who has something—often of little or no substance—to say about *every* item. The Gadfly usually begins with a semi-apology for his or her verbiage in the form of a phrase like, "Maybe it's just me, but . . ." I've sat through lots of sessions with characters like this and have resisted the temptation to jump up and say, "It *is* you. Just shut up for a while and let the rest of us negotiate." I've managed to control that impulse and realize that the Gadfly is relatively harmless. The Gadfly may slow things down, but note that in all that verbiage, there just may lurk a sound idea.

Listen and respond selectively to the Gadfly. Instead of engaging your "automatic shutoff" (see Chapter 7), and even though it is somewhere between difficult and highly exasperating, you should listen to the Gadfly. While these characters tend to make the rest of us roll our eyes heavenward, sometimes buried among their excess verbiage are good ideas and sound positions. Like most people who talk too much, they are only searching for an audience. Listening and responding to their ideas will not only give them an audience but also go a long way toward converting those Gadflies into effective participants and even allies, no matter on which side of the negotiating table they are seated.

The Mad Bomber

The Mad Bomber is the person who is there to disrupt. He or she is mad (either crazy or angry) and a bomber in the sense of wanting to hurl a verbal bombshell that will throw things completely off course or even get people angry enough to leave the negotiating table. Unlike the Bully, the Mad Bomber isn't trying to gain an advantage; he or she is just there to disrupt and even end the negotiations if possible.

The best thing you can do when dealing with the Mad Bomber is to simply let this character fizzle out. Let the Mad Bomber have his or her say and don't interrupt. Allow a strategic silence to pass; then calmly state the goal of the session and declare that you intend to continue the negotiation session. Don't permit the Mad Bomber to interrupt once you regain the floor until you have restated the goals of the session and your intention to continue. By not interrupting during the delivery of the Mad Bomber's attack, you gain the right to say. "Don't interrupt! You were allowed to speak, and now it's my turn!" Then take back the floor and resume the negotiation process. If the Mad Bomber attempts to continue, let him or her talk for ten or so seconds, and then, beginning with the Mad Bomber's name (beginning an interruption with the speaker's name has the effect of a verbal stun gun; even the angriest person will *momentarily* stop talking), restate your determination to continue and enlist both sides. For example, "Richard, while you may want to disrupt our movement toward agreement, the best interests of everyone here are served by reaching that agreement." Remember, an essential ingredient in all negotiation is to keep talking. These strategies plus an appeal to *both* sides to continue should neutralize the Mad Bomber.

The Showboater

The Showboater is the team member who plays a secondary role in the session but feels that he or she should have a larger role. While such characters exist on every team, they don't usually pose a threat to the proceedings unless antagonized. Their statements may be on or off target in the session, but they feel they must have something to say. The tip-off in recognizing Showboaters is that their statements usually contain references to their own experiences, for example, "In my more than twenty years with the company, I've found that . . . ," or other references to past history or other negotiation sessions. At other times the Showboater may engage in a bit of name-dropping, for instance, mentions of a recent lunch with the CEO or a long-past award or distinction.

When dealing with a Showboater, say thanks, recognize him or her, and move on. The Showboater is simply in search of recognition.

Maybe he or she *would* have been an effective team leader or perhaps is an authority on the subject under negotiation but got shifted to a secondary slot. Showboaters are not harmful but can become so if they don't get the recognition they seek. Resist the temptation to quiet the Showboater with remarks such as "We know that, Bill, but you're getting us off the track . . ." or similar dismissive remarks.

Instead, let the Showboater talk. If this character is on your team, you can even ask the Showboater to expand upon his or her remarks. Include the Showboater in the discussion. If the Showboater is on the other team's side and the other team leader makes the mistake of dismissing him or her, ask the Showboater a question such as "Who else worked with you on that management task force?"

It's relatively easy to make the Showboater an ally, no matter which team he or she is on. However, failure to provide that recognition will deprive you of the contributions he or she can make. If the Showboater is on the other team's side and the other team leader has made the mistake of being dismissive, your recognizing the Showboater will gain you an ally or at least go a long way toward silencing a potential antagonist.

Johnny (or Judy) One-Note

It's almost as if these characters were hit on the head with a book at an early age and its contents seeped into their brains. I refer to the one-issue negotiators who keep trying to refocus the proceedings into one area or issue or revisit an issue after it's been settled. Their remarks usually sound like this: "It's still about the numbers [or the office space, or the schedule, or the team sizes, or the benefit package]. And unless we pay closer attention to that issue, we can't possibly come to a useful agreement."

Another tactic of Judy or Johnny One-Note is to link the proceedings to history with a remark like "Remember, the agreement we arrive at here today is something we'll be living with for a long time, so we'd better make sure that the budget reflects . . ." In other words, if I can't get you to focus on my issue with my constant nagging, I'll try linking it to history or the future or company tradition or some important theme that will make my concern larger than it should be.

The best thing to do with the One-Noters is to agree and move on: "Judy, I appreciate your concern and even dedication to this issue; everyone here is equally concerned about the budget, but both sides have made it clear that they are satisfied with the results of the discussion. With everyone's agreement, I'll proceed." As you make this statement, make eye contact with all others present but avoid eye contact with Judy or Johnny One-Note. This is an effective means of nonverbally discouraging the continuation of the One-Noter's efforts, which you can use repeatedly.

As I've said in other contexts, there are no magic-bullet phrases in negotiation. If your use of an agree-and-move-on strategy isn't successful, it may become necessary to segregate Johnny or Judy One-Note and his or her issue by providing them with a separate forum. Late in the proceedings, assuming your attempts to agree and move on have not had the desired effect and the One-Noter's interruptions and persistence are disruptive, it's time to segregate the issue. Here is how it's done: "Judy [Johnny], all of us know of your deep commitment to the issue you have raised so often. Since it is an important issue, I propose a special single-issue meeting after today's session, which I'd like any interested parties to attend. This will be a special session to deal with just this issue."

While you have given Judy or Johnny his or her own forum, you have also marginalized this character and the issue. More important, you can now be more vigorous in cutting off discussion on that issue, since this disruptive character has been given his or her own forum.

The Chorus

At the opera, they stand in the back and add their vocal oomph to crucial scenes. In negotiation, the Chorus is the support staff who sit in the second row of chairs along the wall, take notes, pass notes, and may have little or a lot to do with the outcome of negotiations. In some settings the heavy hitters or real decision makers place themselves in those secondary seats or enter and exit at various times.

Before you deal with the Chorus, be sure to identify *all* the opposing team's cast members. One of the major keys to success in any communicative setting is to know your audience. Your effectiveness as a negotiator is enhanced by knowing as much as you can about just who makes up the Chorus. Maybe they are there as key support staff or maybe they are there just for the sake of appearances, much as the Enron folks once filled phony trading floors with receptionists and the like to convey an atmosphere of activity.

Don't ignore the Chorus. As negotiations begin, try to have *everyone*—not just the key players—in the room introduced to give you an idea of just who is in the cast. Also be sure to include all the team members as much as possible. For example, whenever material is distributed, make sure there are enough copies for the members of the Chorus. Your inclusion of the Chorus will pay off in later sessions if Chorus members move to the front row. Alternatively, if the Chorus includes some hidden decision makers, you will have impressed them with your thoroughness and attention to detail. Even if you're unsuccessful in your attempts to find out *exactly* who the Chorus members are, any attempts to obscure their identities will also be revealing. (You may have just found the *real* decision makers.)

Handling Nonverbal Abuse

We have all heard of verbal abuse in various contexts. Nonverbal abuse consists of tricks played against you in both formal and informal negotiations to distract, aggravate, or somehow throw you off balance. Here are some examples:

The Timekeeper

The Timekeeper is the person on the other team who begins glaring at his watch every few seconds as you speak as if to say, "This is a waste of my time. How long can it continue?" Variations on the Timekeeper include a person who obviously asks a colleague the time and one who resets his or her watch or indicates to a colleague with a finger on the watch face that time is a big concern.

Begin by ignoring the Timekeeper's behavior. It is meant to distract you, and it shouldn't. However, if the room is small enough that the Timekeeper is beginning to draw an audience, stop suddenly. Once everyone is looking your way, look directly at the Timekeeper and inquire, "Do we need to take a recess?" In this manner, you will regain control of the session in that moment or have your audience's undivided attention after a brief recess, which will have given everyone a break and neutralized the Timekeeper.

The Scribe

At some point in the deliberations, you may find yourself making a crucial point when a member of the opposing team begins writing or punching the keyboard of his or her laptop at a furious pace in reaction to something you have said. At least you *think* it's in reaction to something you have said.

The solution to dealing with the Scribe lies in that last sentence. You *think* his or her behavior is in reaction to something you have said. The fact is, you don't *know* why the sudden burst of writing is taking place. It might be in reaction to something you've proposed. It might also be a lunch order or a letter that begins with the words "Dear Mommy, I can't believe I'm sitting at a conference table with all these important people." A good rule in life as well as in negotiation is not to worry about the things you can't control. Ignore the Scribe. Besides, he's not listening to much of what you have to say!

The Optician and Friends

The Optician is the person who not only removes his or her glasses but also decides to give them a thorough cleaning as you make your most important point. His or her friends include the Yawner, the Pencil Tapper, the Wallet Emptier, and the occasional Narcoleptic. All of these characters, as their names suggest, engage in behaviors to distract and disrupt your train of thought and your very effectiveness as a negotiator.

Sometimes these behaviors occur randomly or even out of an appropriate degree of boredom in a long negotiation session. At other times, they are meant to distract and disrupt. The rule is to ignore them to every extent possible. Remember, if you engage one of these characters and win (i.e., you stop the distracting behavior), you have gotten that one listener back, but in exchange you have lost everyone else.

However, if the behavior is distracting to everyone and there's really no point in continuing, take a break, but avoid making reference to the distracting behavior. An alternative is reminding everyone that a scheduled break is approaching. This way, if your distracting friend is engaging in distracting behavior out of fatigue, you will have informed him or her that a break is at hand. This isn't a high school classroom where you get to play the saber-witted teacher who embarrasses an errant class member back into the fold of listeners. This is a negotiation session where embarrassing a colleague on either side of the table is a poor option and should be avoided.

External Distractions

Not all of the distractions in negotiation come from the people in the room. Sometimes the surroundings do a more thorough job of disrupting negotiations. The usual include construction noise, a pesky audio system, noisy air-conditioning, no air-conditioning, a catering service that decides to wheel in lunch as talks reach a crucial state, or even the wail of sirens for those who do business in an urban setting.

A general rule with distractions is to ignore them until they become disruptive. Beyond that, environmental distractions are managed in two ways: First, anticipate and prevent environmental distractions. Audio systems should be thoroughly checked *before* the negotiation session starts, and ventilation problems, strict and specific instructions to the catering staff, and any other environmental oddity can and should be handled in advance.

However, distractions such as construction noise, alarms, or any condition that has the participants no longer engaged in the negotiation process must be managed before negotiations proceed. Cell phones and beepers should be switched off. Negotiations with teams that are only half listening will produce disagreement or a flawed agreement at best! The more distractions you can stop before they start, the better and more productive the negotiation session will be for both sides as they work toward agreement.

Summary

While this chapter has presented a host of strategies for dealing with the cast of occasionally disruptive characters that inhabit the negotiating table, it is important to remember that *all* of these characters are not going to be present at the same time in any one negotiation session. As a general rule, while there may be disagreement on the issue under negotiation, the emergence of characters that engage in disruptive behavior may actually be a sign that you're doing well. The common thread among all these strategies is to remain calm, employ your strategies, and remember: In negotiation and particularly in dealing with difficult people, the one who talks the loudest loses!

Key Thoughts and Takeaway Points

Keep your cool. While this chapter presents tactics for managing the disruptive characters and personalities that may seek to sabotage a negotiation session, the bottom line on all of these strategies is to place yourself in the eye of this verbal hurricane and *remain calm*. This is the one sure way to remain focused on the major product of negotiation—*reaching agreement*!

Quiet is cool! Loud isn't. Furthermore, on the subject of keeping your cool, it has been my experience in observing negotiators that the one who talks the loudest loses. That loss comes in the form of giving up some all-important credibility—both their own and their teams'. Further, that bluster is often followed by the need to back away from the obnoxious outburst with an apology or even some form of concession. Ultimately, the one who talks the loudest loses!

Bad behavior can be good—a good indicator of progress, that is. The emergence of difficult people or behaviors in a negotiation should not always be viewed as a negative. It is very likely a sign that you are making progress in getting to an agreement that is close to the other side's "ouch point," the outer limits of the terms to which they are likely to agree.

———————

CHAPTER FIVE

Managing the Negotiation Environment

AT-A-GLANCE SUMMARY
Such factors as *when* and *where* you negotiate can make a real difference in the results of the session. This chapter examines formal and informal negotiation and shows you how to manage, not just time and place, but *all* of the environmental factors that can influence the outcome of negotiations. It includes valuable information on everything from seating arrangements to the importance of the so-called ritual conversation that often precedes serious talks.

This chapter is about managing the negotiation environment to create an atmosphere that facilitates agreement. Many of the environmental factors that support or detract from success (time, place, surroundings, etc.) are most applicable to formal negotiations simply because the participants are likely to spend a considerable amount of time in that environment. Therefore, a positive outcome in formal negotiations is best served by elaborate preparations and structuring. Not only do formal negotiations involve complex matters, but they are also often very visible, conducted in the presence of a large number of interested parties or their representatives. Formal negotiations may even involve media exposure when there is widespread public interest in the outcome.

In contrast, informal negotiations, which are discussed in the latter half of this chapter, happen on the spur of the moment. While lacking in elaborate planning, informal negotiations do require prior thought and strategy if you are to get the result you want.

Managing the Formal Negotiation Environment

In the case of formal negotiations, planning includes such elements as the time and place as well as who will get to sit at the table. With proper planning, the tensions and disruptions that are often a part of formal negotiations can be minimized so that everyone can focus on reaching an outcome favorable to both sides. Following are some considerations for managing a formal negotiation session toward that favorable outcome.

When to Negotiate

A few factors go into the decision of when to negotiate. First, to what kind of schedule is everyone accustomed? For example, medical and engineering personnel are used to starting their days at 7 AM and might welcome an early start. However, if you want to raise tensions, try telling the executive committee of the musicians' union that you'd like to start at 7 AM!

Consider the audience in selecting a start time. Don't forget to factor in time differences and travel schedules. Those who have traveled east across a time zone or two will appreciate and perform better in a later session. Those who made the same journey in the opposite direction probably won't mind an early start. The point here is to consider the comfort of *everyone* involved in order to make things proceed as smoothly as possible.

Where to Negotiate

Formal negotiations should be held on neutral territory, neither your office nor theirs. If you disagree, just think about the sports tenet of the home-court advantage. The fact is that when a team is playing in their home arena, surrounded by their loudly cheering fans, they tend to win more often. If negotiations are to be held in your offices, the other side is likely to feel like the traveling team. Stripped of the home-court advantage, they'll play—or in this case, negotiate—harder than normal in order to overcome any perceived disadvantage. Start with a truly level playing field (which will be to your ultimate advantage) and hold negotiation sessions at a mutually agreed upon location.

Another factor that works against you in negotiating on your home turf is your degree of accessibility. In conducting corporate seminars, I am often asked whether I'd prefer to hold a session on- or off-site. Invariably I state my preference for an off-site location. At times, either circumstances or bean counters prevail and the session is held there at "headquarters." The result is a day punctuated by interruptions for matters that could have waited, but since you are there on the premises, the interruptions will continue despite your instructions to the contrary.

In negotiations, momentum toward agreement is an important building block of success. Your increased accessibility as a result of conducting a session on your home turf is only going to have a negative effect on that all-important momentum. Being on neutral territory creates a degree of privacy and focus for *both* sides that, especially in the presence of complex issues, facilitates reaching an agreement.

First Class or No Frills?

The impression created by the negotiation environment matters, but don't overdo it. In Jonathan Harr's 1995 book, *A Civil Action*, an attorney from a small and nearly bankrupt firm is trying to win a large settlement from a huge conglomerate. The conglomerate is represented by a highly prosperous and well-regarded law firm. In order to disguise his limited means, the attorney arranges for a settlement conference in an ornate hotel ballroom complete with an opulent breakfast buffet, as if to suggest he usually did business in these surroundings. The stunt backfired. The opposing counsel ignored the elaborate spread, gruffly stated his position, and walked out, stopping only to stuff a pastry in his pocket. The nearly bankrupt attorney ended up with no settlement offer, a whopping hotel bill, and information he could have gotten by phone.

While that attorney may have gone overboard, it's still true that the surroundings do set the tone for negotiations. As such, they should be comfortable, centrally located, and in an atmosphere that *both* sides will find conducive to productivity. If you are negotiating upward (the small firm trying to snare the bigger fish), make the negotiation surroundings something to which *they* are accustomed. You may fly into town on a coach ticket, but make sure the negotiation setting is at least business class.

In contrast, if you are a member of the management team negotiating with union representatives and trying to minimize a wage increase, having the session at the revolving restaurant atop the tallest building in town will work against you.

Work in an atmosphere that makes neither team uncomfortable. Have private adjournment spaces at the ready and all the communicative and culinary amenities to which both sides are accustomed. Use the environment to set the tone, and remember that extremes of opulence or penury will work against you *and* your credibility.

Places, Everyone!

This theatrical cue, heard just before the curtain goes up, is also an important cue in negotiation. Where one sits in a conference room is often a big deal. Places at the negotiating table are often symbolic of power and prestige, or the lack of them. Negotiations are typically held in conference rooms in which the CEO or other head honcho sits at the head of the table near the most expensive painting. Your level of importance is proportionate to your distance from the head of the table.

If negotiators choose their own seats, the team leaders will take positions at either end of the table, with the teams sitting opposite each other. The distance between the team leaders should be prevented, as it presents two problems. First, being at opposite ends of a conference table causes them to speak louder than they would in normal conversation. This facilitates and even encourages raised voices. If things heat up (and remember, you are there to settle a disagreement), you are that much closer to a needlessly loud exchange. When the team leaders get loud, so will everyone else, and your negotiation session is likely to become a shouting match. Second, the distance makes it more difficult for the team leaders to read and react to such nonverbal nuances as facial expressions or even a glance that might signal agreement.

The Double Last Supper Arrangement

Here is my strategy for neutralizing the polarizing effect of the typical conference room and lessening the physical distance between the key players. In the da Vinci painting *The Last Supper,* Christ sat in the center of the table and his team members (the Apostles) sat on either side of him. At the negotiation table, you should borrow that arrangement, that is, team leaders at the center, facing each other, and their team members next to them on either side. This setup resembles a pair of *Last Supper* paintings facing each other. This seating arrangement reduces the hopelessly hierarchical seating arrangement of the typical conference table and facilitates a quieter, more results-oriented session.

Another way of further controlling the seating arrangements and making sure no one occupies the heads of the table is to remove the chairs from either end. You may want to place refreshments at the ends to make things difficult for those who might try to rearrange your established setup. Place cards can be used for the maximum degree of control over the seating arrangements. This way, issues specialists from each side can be minimally distant from one another. For example, *your* accountants should sit near *their* accountants, *your* marketing people near *their* marketing people, and so on. All of these moves will mean a quieter session in which everyone can hear everyone else, everyone speaks more quietly, and counterparts from opposite sides of the table can easily share information, even handing documents across the table.

A couple of additional environmental notes: If you are stuck with a very large negotiating space in which the participants are so far apart as to make conversation difficult, place well-located and modulated microphones about the room so that people can speak in a normal tone of voice. Concerning furniture, if at all possible, have fixed rather than swivel chairs. This keeps the participants focused on one another and the issues and makes it more difficult to signal some degree of displeasure or disagreement by literally turning away from the discussion.

The Dinner Party Effect

Have you ever noticed how the number of people at a dinner determines how the conversation will flow? For example, six people or fewer can have a single conversation. However, if the number gets to eight, a single conversation becomes more difficult. Get ten people at a table, and if one person speaks and nine people listen, it's no longer a conversation but rather a meeting punctuated by an occasional bite to eat. To prevent the dinner party from becoming a meeting, what usually happens after a few remarks from the host is that the group fragments into a series of smaller conversations. Such conversational fragmentation is okay at dinner but can spell disaster for negotiations.

In formal negotiations, to keep things on track and prevent fragmentation from taking hold, spokespersons should be limited to three—certainly no more than four—with each spokesperson having expertise in a designated specialty. For example, in a complex negotiation situation, there may be an expert on finance, another on production, another on engineering, and so forth, so that there is a designated spokesperson from each area. These should be the primary negotiators, along with a team leader or chief spokesperson.

If additional support staff are needed, they can be seated in the room but should be located away from the table and called upon only as needed. This way, the negotiation has the chance of taking on the atmosphere of an intimate dinner party dominated by a single conversation—*one* conversation geared toward agreement, rather than an aimless gabfest. Generally, negotiating teams should be as small as possible, with little or no imbalance between the teams. The extent to which you can manage these environmental factors will speed things along on the road to reaching that agreement.

Structuring Formal Negotiations

Ritual Conversation

At the beginning of the session, the teams enter the room, partake of some refreshments, and begin to take their places around the table.

Even before someone says something like "Let's get down to business and get started," however, the process has already gotten under way with an important part of any business meeting, be it a sales call, job interview, or negotiation session—*ritual conversation.*

In some cultures, business is conducted only *after* lengthy dinners, ceremonial teas, attendance at operas or sporting events, and various other social activities intended to create an atmosphere conducive to doing business. The American shortcut through all of these behaviors takes place in the form of ritual conversation. It usually consists of such banalities as the weather, the journey to the meeting, restaurant recommendations, or news events of the day.

In negotiation, ritual conversation should be viewed as a necessity rather than a necessary evil. Your ability to engage in this polite conversational fluff is an opportunity to show that you have a friendly side. Even if portions of the negotiations become heated, those sitting across from you will know that you have another side—an important piece of information as the negotiations proceed.

While it is the purpose of this book to help you become a better negotiator and not necessarily to enhance your conversational skills, for the conversationally challenged, let me pass along a simple secret of making small talk: Get those in your midst talking about their favorite subject—*themselves*! Instead of worrying about what to say, just have a few stock questions at hand: "How was your trip here? Did you have any trouble finding the conference center?" "Have you been with the company a long time?" "Will you be in town for the big game? Who's your favorite team?" *Any* of these will do to get you on the road to a few minutes of typical ritual conversation. The rule in ritual conversation is to keep it light, to keep it real, and, as your parents told you, *to stay away from religion and politics*!

Defining the Problem

Once the ritual conversation subsides, it's time to get down to business. That means defining the problem or deciding *exactly* what's being negotiated. You can't arrive at an agreement if you don't know where the disagreement lies, so your initial task should be to arrive at a statement of the problem as well as a series of areas to be negotiated.

If possible, the problem or objectives statement should be drawn up in advance, with the basic content agreed to by both sides. This should be a concise statement of the purpose of the negotiations, such as:

> To arrive at an agreement of terms for a labor contract between the management of Krylex Manufacturing and the members of the International Federation of Krylex Workers. The agreement to be in force for a period of three years beginning ninety days from the conclusion of these talks and subject to ratification by a simple majority of the union membership.
>
> The items to be negotiated are:
> 1. Revision of day-care-center eligibility rules
> 2. Employee meal allowance allotments
> 3. Proposed increase in personal-day allocation
> 4. Evaluation and adjustment of dental plan
> 5. Cost-of-living allowances for the retirement plan
> 6. Establishment of a tiered salary structure for professional staff
> 7. Evaluation and adjustment of current salary schedules

The objectives statement also could look like this:

> The objective of the current negotiations is the development of an agreement to continue with Craymor Computers as the primary supplier for this company.
>
> The items to be negotiated are:
> 1. Increased employee support and training
> 2. Priority assignment of new models
> 3. Use of outside suppliers for training support
> 4. Evaluation and adjustment of the service/support agreement
> 5. Shortened delivery schedules
> 6. Pricing adjustments for new units shipped

Once the list is established, it should be distributed to everyone present as an agenda and guide to the running order of the items to be negotiated. Whether the statement of objectives and list of items are prearranged or not, they should be the initial agenda items for discussion for two reasons. First, it will mean that *everyone* has a clear idea of what the goals are. Second, while the statement of objectives and items list are important, their general nature permits revision by those at the table without the need to make any real concessions. Aside from clarifying the issues, the negotiations now begin in an area where everyone can agree (or disagree) without cost or consequence regarding actual issues under consideration. The flexibility shown and any agreement made on this preliminary task will further set the tone for the negotiations to follow and will demonstrate that those present are capable of agreement—another step in building momentum toward a final agreement.

Visual Reinforcement

One technique that I have found effective in moving negotiations along is to post the objectives statement in a place visible to both teams and to post a list of items settled once they are finalized. Whether it is a simple collection of flip-chart pages or projected graphics in more elaborate surroundings, this posting serves as a visible reminder of progress and reinforces an atmosphere in which agreement is being achieved.

Start with the Easy Stuff

A Broadway musical doesn't open with its big number. Instead, a series of songs and plotlines are introduced, culminating in that big number—complete with full orchestra, chorus, and the highest notes in the score. Similarly, formal negotiations shouldn't begin with the major issue. Negotiators should have time to warm up and get to know one another, becoming acclimated to one another's behaviors, emotions, and approaches to the issues. This is best accomplished by tackling some of the minor items first. Once the normal give-and-take of the negotiations has been established on the lesser items, a level of momentum and mutual trust will help the session proceed.

Occasionally in my seminars, I run into some disagreement on this approach; participants tell me, "Putting off the tough stuff to the end is beating around the bush! You should dive into the major issues right away and let the best person win!" I would remind those of you who are tempted toward that approach that this is negotiation, not a televised wrestling match. The goal is agreement, not victory—settlement, not theater. So begin with the minor items and get things rolling. This approach will make the going easier when you get to the crucial issues.

The Formal Negotiation Structure

After the objectives of the session are determined and the specific issues to be negotiated are decided, formal negotiations should follow a four-step sequence for each of those issues: (1) position statement, (2) response and initial proposal, (3) discussion, and (4) counteroffer and agreement discussion. This sequence is repeated for each issue or agenda item.

Step #1: Position Statement

In this initial phase, in which the first (and easiest) issue is discussed, if you can, let the other team speak first. The advantage goes to the side that speaks second, since they gain advance information on such items as the emotional state and degree of preparedness of the other side as well as how much disagreement has to be overcome on the journey toward agreement. In negotiations with fewer issues, it pays to go for the "second-speaker" advantage, but in more complex settings an alternating arrangement is fairest and works best.

Step #2: Response and Initial Proposal

During this second phase, each side states their position on the opening agenda item, based primarily on prior preparation and in part in response to what they have heard at the table. Depending on the complexity of the issues, this response portion may be immediate. However, highly complex issues may require a recess during which each team constructs their response. Such recesses should be planned and announced in advance so as not to be confused with one team's making a sudden exit as a reaction to the opposing side's initial statement.

Step #3: Discussion

This period of reaction to the proposal phase of the discussion is where the heart of negotiation takes place. This discussion should have mutually agreed upon time limits for each speaker as well as for the overall session. Such limits can and often are suspended if the group wishes—especially when agreement is near. Setting time limits is an acknowledgment of the principle that the amount of time needed to complete a task expands to fill an interval equal to the amount of time available. It's also a strategy to deal with those who often, out of a love for the sound of their own voices, will spend hours needlessly ruminating over the most trivial of issues.

Step #4: Counteroffer and Agreement Discussion

The counteroffer may arise within the discussion or exist as a distinct portion of the negotiations, preceded by a recess at which this counteroffer is formulated. At this stage, all participants should be made aware that a counteroffer is a signal of a genuine intention of coming to an agreement. By the time the counteroffer phase is reached, each side has given up some checkers in order to get this far. Therefore, the overriding theme of what I call "the agreement discussion" should be an answer to the question "How can we agree?"

These four areas represent the basic cycle of the formal negotiation process. The process can be interrupted, varied, stretched, or even rushed. However, along with the application of many of the strategies described in Chapter 8, this structure will facilitate the attempt to arrive at an agreement advantageous to both sides.

Endgame

In the most complex of negotiations, the key players should set the tone, establish the areas of agreement, and leave the preparation of the formal agreement to support teams. Local culture will determine the degree to which the key players get involved in the minutiae. However, remember that the old maxim "Too many cooks spoil the broth" is as applicable to the negotiation process as it is to the kitchen.

Informal Negotiations

Self-Management in Informal Negotiations

Up to now the focus has been on formal negotiations—those that center on complex issues with consequential and long-lasting outcomes. Informal negotiations, in contrast, are those spur-of-the-moment situations in which you are trying to gain an advantageous outcome in a matter that, while of momentary importance, is usually unrelated to large, life-altering issues. Informal negotiations involve such issues as getting the best price possible on a new car, nailing down the final details of a real estate transaction, or perhaps getting a wholesale price even though you're a retail customer.

Plan Ahead

While informal negotiations are spur-of-the-moment, it doesn't mean they're not expected. For example, you may have been planning to ask for a raise during an afternoon meeting with your boss, but a chance meeting with him or her in the parking lot may provide an even better opportunity for that conversation.

A salesperson in an auto showroom may ask the opportunity-laden question "What can I do to get you to buy now?" and, if you're ready with a response, the outcome is likely to be better than expected. A supplier may call you for a delivery-date approval and instead of responding with the usual yes or no, you should be able to get an earlier date if you're ready to negotiate. In fact, informal negotiations can yield dramatic results because of that element of surprise or spontaneity, but you can gain that advantage only by doing the surprising rather than being the one surprised—a position you can be in only if you plan ahead, know your goals, and are ready to act.

Don't Apologize for Negotiating

In your initial attempts at informal negotiation, you may be hesitant, fearing a negative outcome. That hesitancy is characterized by any hint of apology as you attempt to attain your objective. Whether your target is wearing a three-piece suit or bib overalls, he or she can spot the apologetic negotiator right away, and that negative outcome will be a sure thing.

For example, when talking to someone in authority, if you begin your remarks with "I know you're busy, but if you have a moment I'd like to discuss the possibility . . . ," you might as well not finish the sentence because you've already categorized your request as an interruption. You also labeled your position a "possibility" rather than an outcome, giving the target easy access to the response "Of course it's always a possibility, but just not right now."

When You're About to Get Shot Down, Don't Supply the Bullet

When I encourage people to negotiate, I often hear the response "I couldn't possibly ask for that; he'll just turn me down." If you think that way, you're programming yourself to fail. Entering negotiations with negative expectations means you are likely to provide your target with an excuse to reject your proposal or even to refuse to negotiate.

For example, if you're asking for a discount in a retail establishment, the kind where the merchandise has price tags and even the employees have name tags, don't begin bargaining by saying "I know you don't usually do this sort of thing, but . . ." You've just given the salesperson his or her response, which you'll realize when you hear the words "You're exactly right; we don't do this sort of thing." Instead, be direct and unapologetic. What you should have said is "Who do I see to get a discount on this item?" Even if you get turned down, let the sales staff come up with their own reason; it might be so full of holes that you'll be in a better position to negotiate further.

In contrast, if you are the target of a hesitant or apologetic negotiator, you can preserve your advantage by using their hesitancy to end the discussion. In informal negotiations, absent the structure and environment that have so much influence on the outcome, *how* you say what you want becomes much more crucial, especially given the spur-of-the-moment nature of the negotiation. Any sign of hesitancy or self-doubt will be pounced on or at least noticed by your target and used against you. Since words become so much more crucial in these situations, following are some specific examples of the kind of verbal self-management that will enhance your effectiveness in informal negotiation:

If they say . . .	You should say . . .
"I was hoping that . . ."	"There just is no hope on this. . ."
"If it's possible, I'd like a raise . . ."	"And if it was possible, I'd like you to have one, but . . ."
"I know you'd be bending the rules, but . . ."	"And you know that even if I wanted to, I couldn't make an exception . . ."
"I have an unusual request . . ."	"As you said yourself, it's unusual, and I'm sorry to say that . . ."

In informal negotiation, never give your target the means to dismiss you. Avoid such weasel words as "might," "possibly," and "hopefully." They're a dead giveaway that you expect to fail. Don't apologize with openings like "I'm sorry to bother you, but I was wondering if . . . ," and don't give your target an excuse to say no with openings like "I know you don't usually . . ." Think of such excuses as conversational boomerangs. Not only will they come back quickly, but they'll have very negative results.

Ten Key Statements for Informal Negotiations

Since informal negotiations often involve less crucial objectives than formal negotiations, you can afford to be more verbally aggressive. Assuming you can go elsewhere to get what you want and a negative outcome will not be that costly to you, following are some aggressive, results-oriented openers:

> "This is unacceptable." (regarding price, a product, something the target wants you to sign)

> "You've got to do better than this."

> "What's the very best you can do?" Follow up with "I'm sure you can still do better."

> "If you're saying you can't make an exception, who can?"

> "We both know exceptions are made all the time . . . so what about . . . ?"

> "We both know this price is way off."

> "I'm ready to buy right now, but only if the price is right."

> "I know you're making an effort, but it's just not enough."

"I wasn't even considering this, but at the right price . . ."

"I don't really like it, but I'm willing to settle if the price comes down."

Aggressive Works; Obnoxious Doesn't

Thus far, I've encouraged you to be direct and aggressive. Both these behaviors will gain you an advantage in negotiations, especially in informal situations. But being aggressive and direct doesn't mean being insulting ("You people have got to be kidding with these prices!") or threatening ("If I don't get what I want, you'll be hearing from my lawyers!"), or raising the decibel level high enough make those around you think about calling security. In both formal and informal negotiations, the quietly insistent, self-assured, polite negotiator gets better results than the bully every time. When you negotiate, have the facts, and in both formal and informal negotiations, deliver that information quietly and deliberately. Being full of sound and fury while short on facts will get you nothing. Aggressive works. Obnoxious doesn't.

Summary

This is the chapter to review before beginning formal negotiations. When the stakes are high and the issues are complex, such factors as the schedule, the location, and even the seating arrangements of the sessions may initially sound trivial. However, don't make the mistake of trivializing the environmental factors. Set the tone and use the strategies and structures of this chapter to reach agreement rather than victory.

Key Thoughts and Takeaway Points

Comfort is key. The very nature of negotiation means that it takes place in the presence of disagreement. Discomfort makes it more difficult to remain focused in any communicative situation, from a meeting to a sales presentation, but *especially* in negotiation. Therefore, the setting should be one in which comfort is maximized. Comfort means placing the participants in surroundings in which they can function at their best. This translates directly into environmental factors that range from the seating arrangements to the time of day, even to the scheduling of breaks and meals. Make the session too long, too short, or too crowded, the surroundings too opulent or too bare-bones, and you will impede and lengthen the path to agreement.

Ritual conversation helps. Dismissing the value of the ritual conversation that often occurs among participants is a mistake. While discussing the results of "the big game," the weather, the flight into town, or other such banalities may seem trivial, such banter lets the participants see one another as themselves rather than as adversaries and thus facilitates a more civil atmosphere for the main event.

Avoid being apologetic or expressing doubt about your position. This usually comes in the form of such phrases as "I know our numbers seem a bit high, but . . ." While you may see this as an attempt at reasonableness, the other side will see it for what it really is—an apology for the inadequacy of your position. Be they the result of fatigue or that all-too-human need to be liked, such statements will cost you.

It's not me; it's this company. Another form of apology and weakness is the tendency to separate yourself from a position to which you are not fully committed with an attitude that says, "It's not me; it's them." If such an attitude is another attempt at being well liked, you've succeeded, but you've also succeeded in weakening your negotiating strength on that issue.

CHAPTER SIX

The Language of Negotiation

AT-A-GLANCE SUMMARY
It's been said that people judge you by the words you use. This is especially true when you negotiate. This chapter gives you guidance on making the kind of language choices that will help you achieve your negotiations objective. You'll also learn how to keep the peace in a heated session as well as how to read the hidden messages that are often unwittingly sent by the other side.

In negotiation, the language choices you make not only set the tone for the session but can speed negotiations along toward agreement, slow them down, or even halt progress. Observation of the language choices made by the other side will often provide clues to their feelings on the matter under negotiation. Responding strategically to that language can help you achieve your goals. This chapter is about sending the right signals and saying the things that will move people toward agreement. Since language is also a receptive medium, you'll also learn how to better judge the other side by the words they use.

Language gives strong clues to such factors as commitment to a position and, therefore, how strongly the speaker is willing to advocate that position. But such clues can be subtle, and you may miss them if you're not listening for them. For example, when schoolkids talk about their grades, they say things like "I got an A" or "I got a B." But when they haven't done quite so well, the language they choose to express this misfortune isn't "I got a C" but rather "He [or she] gave me a C." What's being expressed here, in addition to some bad news, is a shift in the responsibility for that bad news from the student to the teacher.

A version of the same shift takes place in negotiation. Listen to the pronouns used by your opposition in formal negotiation. If personal pronouns are rare and the opposing team uses references to "the company" instead of "we," it can signal discomfort on the other side. This subtle language signals an attempt to gain some distance from a position in which the negotiators lack conviction—a useful piece of information as you pose alternatives to that position.

Let's Work Together

Minimizing the Hatfield-McCoy Effect

You may know the story of the Hatfields versus the McCoys as the mother of all family feuds. Legend has it that for more than a century, these two clans, who lived on opposite sides of the West Virginia–Kentucky border, communicated with bullets rather than words. Let's hope that the situations in which you negotiate will be more peaceful, but the reason you are negotiating is that there is some kind of disagreement to be worked out. No matter what the psychological climate, nonconfrontational, nondivisive language will help create an atmosphere in which agreement is more likely to take place. Following are some examples of good choices (*inclusive*) and poor choices (*divisive*) for the negotiation session:

Inclusive	Divisive
All of us	Our side / Your side
We	Your, you people, you
Both sides can agree that	If the opposition insists
We need to get closer on	You're way off when it comes to
We	I (instead, always use "we" to refer to your team)
Everyone here	Each of you
All of us	They (the other side as third person)

We believe that	It is our side's position that
Let's agree on	Okay, you win on that, but
How would we all feel if	If your side is willing to go along with

Notice that each of the inclusive language choices is devoid of references to sides. This minimizes the Hatfield-versus-McCoy or us-versus-them tone that may initially pervade the negotiation setting. Also note the avoidance of positions and sides in favor of the much more inclusive "all of us" and the stronger "let's agree on." Inclusive language as a strategy sets a tone that is conducive to agreement. Sure, agreement is possible without the use of inclusive language, but if the goal is agreement, the use of inclusive language will speed the process and minimize the posturing and stridency that can characterize negotiations.

Inclusive language as a strategy need not be practiced by both sides. Even when one negotiating team is antagonistic, the other negotiating team's use of inclusive language as a tactic will neutralize the force of that antagonism. The alternative is that if *they* come in angry, *you* have to get angry, after which *everyone* has to calm down. Only then can serious and productive negotiation begin to take place. The use of inclusive language breaks this cycle and makes real negotiation and agreement come sooner.

Asking the Right Questions

Reaching agreement is also facilitated by asking the right questions; the key questions are "How can we agree?" and "How can we get closer on this issue?"

Simply asking yes-or-no questions creates barriers to agreement. For example, the simple and seemingly innocent question "Can we agree on this?" asked in reference to a problematic issue is most likely to produce a resounding "No!" Such questions produce little or no information, fail to stimulate discussion, and reinforce the presence of disagreement.

In negotiation, a question type preferable to the yes-or-no question is the how-or-what question, for example, "*How* can we get closer on this?" or "*What* can we do to gain some movement on this issue?" or "*What* will make this a win-win situation for all of us?" With each of these questions, instead of evoking a simple yes-or-no response, you encourage discussion and further examination of the issues.

Build Bridges Instead of Walls

The whole reason for negotiations is to settle a disagreement—to arrive at some middle ground. Otherwise, disagreements are settled by arguments or even litigation, in which there are winners and losers. Arguments can be considered walls that need to be broken down and even destroyed before the disagreement is settled. Negotiation is a process of building bridges, which bring the sides closer together without the destructive exchanges that characterize arguments. Such bridges are best built with language that is open-ended and provides options rather than the closed-ended language of the ultimatum. Following are some examples of ways to disagree and yet provoke discussion, as well as examples of the wrong way to do things—building linguistic walls instead of bridges:

Closed-Ended (Walls)	Open-Ended (Bridges)
"That's impossible!"	"It's really difficult to meet those terms."
"You're way off!"	"That's a big difference, which would be tough to overcome."
"That's an insult."	"Sure, we want your business, but that's way over our target price."
"Take it or leave it!"	"That is a firm offer that we'd be happy to clarify so there's no misunderstanding."
"Are you kidding?"	"We take every offer seriously, but this one is really in need of improvement."

Putting up verbal walls will create more heat than light. Don't hesitate to disagree in negotiation but, in so doing, build bridges. This way you'll increase the level of discussion instead of the blood pressure of those across the table from you.

Handling Numbers in Negotiation

Much of negotiation, especially in business settings, centers on numbers. Prices, financing terms, deadlines, contract expirations and extensions, and even solutions to legal disputes are numerical components of negotiations. If the numbers under discussion are of a crucial nature, and they often are, discussion of them should be held off until the final stages of the negotiation.

There is a great deal of discomfort in many quarters when it comes to discussing numbers. How many times have you viewed the jewelry in a store window and noticed that all of the price tags were routinely and strategically hidden from view. (What are they trying to hide and why?) New cars for sale are required by law to have window stickers. Used cars for sale, almost without exception, are not marked with prices, giving me the queasy feeling that the price is going to be as much as the dealer can get out of me.

The key to success in discussing numbers is to replace that discomfort with directness. For example, if you are trying to negotiate a certain price, develop that price including a fair profit. In developing your price, take into account such elements as quantity discounts (which you may want to initially hold back during negotiations), required delivery dates, service agreements, performance incentives, any premium commanded by your reputation or brand name, and so on, and present it directly and without apology. If that price is properly constructed, the negotiated price should approximate your initial estimate.

Ritualistic Bargaining

In most negotiation, there is some ritualistic bargaining on the subject of price. For example, a buyer's corporate culture may make it important for him or her to say, "They wanted $100 per unit, but I was able to get that number down to $85." In preparing for negotiation, part of your task is to anticipate that likelihood of ritualistic bargaining and to build that discount into your price just to take it away. (This is why I suggest initially holding back the quantity discount.)

When you've included the "ritual discount" in your price and the negotiation progresses without that discount actually being discussed, be certain to include that discount in the final negotiated price anyway. You might look at this oversight on the part of your opponent as an opportunity, but letting a customer pay 15 percent too much because he or she forgot to raise the point that would have negotiated the discount will work only once. Eventually, the one who should have asked the question that would have triggered the discount will figure out or, even worse, be informed by a competitor that he or she paid too much. Your momentary advantage will taint, if not end, future business with that prospect.

Avoid Numerical Weasel Words

When discussing numbers in general and prices in particular, avoid such phrases as "suggested retail price" or "asking price." Both these phrases, as common as they might be, have a negative impact on your credibility because you are presenting a piece of information and saying, "Here is my price but it's merely *suggested,* so go ahead and make your own suggestion."

The term "suggested retail price" or "manufacturer's suggested retail price" (MSRP) is used by TV infomercial spokespersons who try to pass themselves off as great humanitarians by selling an item with an MSRP of $400 for a mere $69.95! By saying "our MSRP" or using the phrase "asking price," you are revealing an insecurity about pricing policy that those sitting across from you are almost obligated to exploit. In discussing price as the vendor or the potential customer, avoid the weasel words and remember that a fair and direct approach is the key to success.

Avoid Discussing Ranges

Many negotiators make the mistake of mentioning number ranges instead of numbers. For example, never say that the price has to be somewhere between $125,000 and $130,000. In doing so, you've just revealed your *entire* position—from your lowest price to your maximum.

Once a good negotiator knows your pricing range, he or she will seize upon the lower number ($125,000) and work downward, and you'll end up with a much lower price than the $130,000 you might have gotten had you avoided stating a range. Instead of ranges, name your planned and justifiable price and stick with it, at least until it's time to go to your fallback position.

Now, if I'm sitting across the table from you and I'm presented with a single price or deadline, I can only approximate and have no idea how firm your position is. I am therefore less likely to hit the lowest number in your range, simply because you haven't revealed it. Be it deadlines, prices, or any other numerically based negotiation point, you'll always do better by stating individual numbers rather than ranges.

Handling Verbal Violence

People exert control over one another through their manner of expression. That is, if the first participant in a conversation talks quickly and in a loud tone of voice, the response that follows from the next speaker is going to be just as loud and similarly rapid. That's what makes for a heated argument. The first person to speak is angry, and the target of the anger finds it necessary to respond in kind.

Similarly, the language used by the first speaker in a conversation sets the tone, and the next speaker usually responds in kind. For example, if I begin a negotiation session with "I've seen the numbers in your side's proposal, and believe me, you guys are way the hell off. I mean, you must be out of your minds to try and lowball us like that! You must think we're idiots!"

The tendency in most conversations is to respond to the behavior and the emotionally charged language of that statement with something like "If you think we're 'way the hell off,' as you put it, you're sure acting like idiots! The numbers in our proposals are damn good, and you know it."

Thus begins the verbal equivalent of the schoolyard shoving match: You feel compelled to shove back. Why? As any kid would say, "Because he shoved me first!" That reasoning is just as defective at the negotiating table as it is in the schoolyard but unfortunately just as common.

Let's examine what happened here: The other side came in with both barrels blazing. Some mild profanity was hurled at you, and your proposal was ridiculed ("You must be out of your minds!"). Typically, you get angry and respond by repeating their profanity, adding a bit of your own, and go right to the edge with a bit of name-calling: "You're sure acting like idiots!" This is mere posturing, much like in the aforementioned schoolyard. Be it little kids in a playground or a group of people sitting around a negotiating table, things get loud, then maybe even a bit louder and a bit more profane. Finally, someone suggests that everyone calm down and get to the assigned task.

Don't Get into a Shoving Match

In negotiation, you gain the advantage by letting the posturing—and even the profanity—go on, and *never* responding directly to it. Think of the martial arts principle of keeping your opponent off balance. Not responding in kind to the other side's outburst has a similar effect. Instead of getting into a verbal shoving match, take a quick step back, leaving your opponent jousting with air. Here is how the above scene would play out if you refrain from shoving back:

THEIR OPENNING: "I've seen the numbers in your side's proposal, and believe me, you guys are way the hell off! You must think we're idiots!"

YOUR RESPONSE: "That's not the case at all. Actually, the numbers in our proposal were the result of very thorough research, and we'd be happy to explain how we arrived at any of these numbers in detail. Give us an example of a figure that posed a problem."

What happened here was that the other side tried to set the tone—loud and angry. To demonstrate that, they threw in a bit of mild profanity and name-calling. Your nonemotional response successfully rejected the tone they were trying to set, and established that your intent is to negotiate rather than to posture. Let them call names; don't tell them to calm down. Instead, recalibrate the emotional tone with your response.

Keeping Your Cool in the Face of Cursing

Sometimes posturing and anger from the other side come out in the form of profanity—words meant to offend and anger you. Every culture has its verbal escape valves, words that are usually taboo in the general politeness of formal negotiations. If your opposition hurls a string of "hells," "damns," and much worse at you, the tendency is to respond with your own gush of profanity. If you respond this way, however, you are out of the realm of negotiation and into that of the verbal duel. How should you have handled this onslaught? Don't try to win. You can't. If you have the presence of mind not to leap into the verbal sewer with those sitting across the table, also steer clear of responses like "Watch your language! I'm not here to take this kind of crap from you!"

Maybe you're justified in shoving back, but exactly what have you accomplished from a tactical point of view? Nothing at all. In your momentary attempt to regain your emotional equilibrium, you have signaled to the other side that they can get you upset—an important piece of information they might take advantage of during a later phase of the negotiations.

Here's another example of what *not* to say when those across the table are doing their best to rattle your cage: "Calm down, and don't speak to me in that tone of voice if you expect to continue these talks."

How do *you* react when someone tells you to calm down? Again, examine exactly what you've accomplished with this verbal warning shot. You've committed the tactical blunder of telling them *exactly* how they can get you to walk out—a very useful piece of information if it's in their interest to end the negotiations!

The strategic response to any verbal outburst is to pause, letting the last echo of the outburst fade, and immediately and matter-of-factly bring the discussion back to the negotiation issue with little or no mention of the opposition's heightened emotional state. Here is a sample response: "There are a lot of issues to focus on, some really difficult. What's best for all of us is to begin to see where we can agree. Let's take a look at . . ."

With this statement, you've clearly demonstrated that verbal pyrotechnics won't have any effect on you or the negotiations. You have also demonstrated your intention of focusing on the issues. Finally, you've avoided getting personal either in the sense of being offended by the outburst or in the sense of feeling it necessary to respond on your opponent's level. We control each other's verbal behavior in a conversation with our tone and language choices. Therefore, when extremes of emotion are loudly expressed, if you respond in the same manner, you are in effect being controlled by the behavior of the other negotiator. In contrast, by not getting loud, you make your opponent's behavior less appropriate and in so doing shift the balance so that you begin to control the behavior of the opposition.

The strategy of not responding and instead bringing the focus back to the issues under negotiation is effective but is sometimes limited by the culture in which you are operating. If getting loud or offensive is totally intolerable to those present, another solution is to take a break or have a cooling-off period.

In calling for that break, be careful not to make direct reference to the heightened emotions in the room, which would let everyone know that your buttons have been pushed. Here is an example of an appropriate response: "Clearly there are deep concerns about these issues that require calm consideration from all sides. Perhaps a recess would be helpful so that we can regroup and continue our work toward a solution." Follow this statement with a strategic silence and a chance to let the other side respond. At a moment like this, *any* kind of agreement is preferable to an impasse or further verbal jousting, even an agreement to temporarily suspend the proceedings.

Unite and Conquer!

I've pointed out numerous times that the purpose of negotiation is to arrive at an agreement. The reason you are sitting at opposite sides of the table is that there is disagreement. As a negotiator, you have a choice: You can push the sides farther apart and intensify the level of disagreement or you can bring the sides closer together and reach that agreement. No matter what the atmosphere, this state of relative unity is where you need to end up.

Language can either delay or encourage settlement. In addition to inclusive language, another control factor at your disposal is the avoidance of emotionally charged language in referring to either the issues or the people in the room. The less emotional your choices, the less emotionally charged the session, resulting in a gathering that generates more light than heat.

Receipt of subpar proposals might elicit emotional reactions saying that the proposals:

- are lousy
- are disgraceful
- are an embarrassment
- are a slap in the face
- are stupid or idiotic
- show total ignorance of our side's position
- show you prefer war over peace
- are just plain dishonest
- are what we expected from people like you

Responses like these aren't going to move the proceedings closer to a point of agreement. Instead of using emotionally charged language, express your disagreement with the proposals in a way that makes the point without pushing the negotiators farther apart than they already are. You might say the proposals:

- are highly problematical
- present major difficulties
- will be really unsettling to . . .
- exclude some major issues
- raise a number of issues
- create a distance between us on . . .

Once you've expressed disagreement calmly, instead of being angered, your opponents are more likely to be listening, especially if a proposal was a test balloon or was presented to see how far you or your side could be pushed. By responding and disagreeing in a restrained manner, you've kept the discussion moving toward agreement while expressing an opposing point of view.

Talk about "It," Not "Them"

A common theme in this discussion about language has been keeping the discussions focused on reaching agreement. Nothing heats up the atmosphere faster than when a member of a negotiating team takes a comment personally or engages in a personal attack on the other side.

A simple, effective, language-based solution to keeping things from getting personal is to always focus your discussion on the issue at hand rather than the people in the room. This means a minimal use of references to "them" and more frequent discussion about "it." For example, "I can't accept that number" becomes "That number is quite a problem."

This tactic also works if you or your team members are the target of an attempt to make the negotiations personal. When you hear comments such as "You know very well as team leader that . . . ," the tendency is to shoot back with "I do not . . ." This response means you've taken the bait and been sidetracked. You are now going down the path of getting personal, which may be momentarily appropriate but has little or nothing to do with arriving at an agreement.

Instead, when you hear comments that begin with "You know that," respond in an issues-based manner, talking about the issue, not you. For example, say, "A closer look at this issue from any perspective makes it clear that . . ." Once again, talk about "it" instead of "you" or "them."

Listen to *Their* Language

Thus far, I have been discussing language strategies you can employ to gain the upper hand in negotiation. But language is both an expressive (what you say) and receptive (what they say) medium. You can gather information about the other side and gain strategic cues if you are attentive to their language choices.

Us or Them?

An opposing team's presentation that is laced with references to "you people" or "our side," is expressing anger or strong disagreement. Angry people have already given up some control, a failure that you can exploit. The opposing team's stance also says that they are approaching the negotiations from a more emotional than logical level, something you can exploit as negotiations near an end.

Answers in Questions

Are those across the table from you making the mistake of asking yes-or-no questions? Don't get boxed in. Questions such as "Are you going to accept this offer or not?" should be met with responses such as "An important matter such as this deserves more than a one-word answer. For example, on the issue of . . ." Begin a discussion of one of the easier issues.

Listen for Ultimatums

"Take it or leave it" is the mark of the Bully or the Bluffer. Don't get trapped into responding on the opposition's terms. Begin with "That's not an appropriate way to approach this issue. For example, on the issue of . . ." Alternatively, begin with an even stronger response: "The all-or-nothing approach being taken here suggests a serious underestimation of our position." Remember: If you really were so powerless that you had to accept an ultimatum, they wouldn't be at the table negotiating with you!

Number Talk Adds Up

If the opposition makes the mistake of talking ranges when discussing numbers, pounce on the most favorable number and negotiate from there. If, for example, you hear that the opposition's lowest price will have to be in the $30,000–$35,000 range, forget the higher number and begin negotiating down from the lower number. Also, be on the lookout for numerical weasel words such as "our *suggested* or *usual* price is . . ." Any such numerical qualifiers from the opposing team are a strong indicator of softness on their proposed numbers or position—a situation you should be ready and willing to exploit.

Summary

I began this chapter by saying that people judge you by the words you use. In negotiation, language sets the tone and speeds things along or causes negotiations to get bogged down in a sea of argument and personal attacks. Once this happens, the goal becomes one of winning instead of reaching agreement. Fights have winners and losers; negotiation has participants and beneficiaries. The language-based strategies contained in this chapter will help steer the situation toward the latter, favorable outcome. Be inclusive, not divisive. Build bridges, not walls.

Observe but don't be controlled by the language behavior of the other side, and agreement will come more quickly and smoothly.

Key Thoughts and Takeaway Points

Build bridges—not walls! Confrontational language creates an atmosphere of combativeness, and in combat, losses are inevitable. Since victory in negotiation is agreement, you should lose such language as "You've got to be kidding!" and all other expressions of indignation or outrage. Instead, the constant theme and question you should ask is "How can we reach agreement on this?"—followed by reasoned and civil discussion.

Keep the numbers real. Bluffing is a time-honored and accepted negotiation tactic in many quarters; but bluffing is also a waste of time. Sure, sometimes it's done for the benefit of an audience, rather than the people present at the negotiation table (for example, elected union leaders may be putting on a show for their constituents), but putting that piece of theater aside, numbers have to be real (as opposed to outlandish) in order for the parties to move toward agreement—so keep them real!

CHAPTER SEVEN

Listen and Learn

AT-A-GLANCE SUMMARY
Success in negotiation comes not only from what you say; what you hear and how you respond can make a difference in outcomes. Yet, research tells us that we retain very little of what we hear and spend a great deal of time in any communicative encounter not listening at all. In negotiations, this flawed listening behavior can produce equally flawed agreements. This chapter shows you how to boost your listening skills and sharpen your focus so that what you hear is closer to what you get.

"How did we ever agree to this?" is a question likely to be asked by the negotiator with poor listening skills. Along with fatigue and the rush to finish, various barriers to effective listening that plague all of us can result in your making an agreement you should have walked away from. This chapter is about how to break down those barriers, particularly in formal negotiations, and better manage your listening skills in order to get a further edge.

Perceptual Barriers to Effective Listening

The Out-Listening Factor

Within every one of us, there is a perceptual trap that causes us to forget or ignore anywhere from a third to one-half of what is said in any spoken communication. This can be especially disadvantageous in negotiation. The problem is that you can think faster than anyone can talk. Studies suggest that you comprehend language nearly *six times* faster than it can be spoken. Therefore, as you listen, what actually happens is that you quickly figure out what the speaker is probably going to say. At that point you think about something else while you half listen for something that recaptures your attention. Think of this as giving someone your *divided* attention. As you listen, this process, which communication theorists call *out-listening*, is repeated over and over.

If you've ever been in a negotiation session or a meeting and found yourself thinking such thoughts such as "Where did he get that ugly tie?" "Was that noise thunder? I hope I closed my car windows!" and yet remained aware of the proceedings, you have experienced the out-listening cycle.

Can you avoid out-listening? Not if you're human. The key to managing the out-listening cycle is in minimizing its effects by catching it *as* it happens to minimize your "time away" from the negotiation issues. Effectively managing the out-listening cycle is one of the keys to never having to say, "How did we ever agree to this?"

Challenge Listening

"Challenge listening" is my term for the selective type of listening you engage in when your sole purpose is to find evidence to use against the speaker or the speaker's team. If that's your only focus, you will actually ignore any information that doesn't fit that purpose. For example, if you have heard that the opposition will be presenting an unreasonable price demand, once you hear their number, you cease listening. Instead of listening, you begin thinking and saying to yourself, "They have some nerve coming in with that price" or "I knew they would be tough, but I didn't think they'd be dishonest as well." The problem with challenge listening as a negotiator is that while your head fills with those "I knew this would happen!" thoughts, you are no longer focused on building a response.

Acceptance Listening

A solution to the problem of challenge listening is what I call "acceptance listening." For example, when you hear a part of the other side's case that is somehow disturbing, such as an outrageous number or a ridiculous proposal, make note of it instead of being overcome by the

"I knew it!" thoughts that preoccupy the challenge listener. Keep listening. It's important to do so because what usually follows the proposal or demand is a justification. For example, they may say, "I know our number seems high, but it's that way because . . ."—and you certainly don't want to miss that!

This justification (which the challenge listener never quite hears) is often a good basis for your response to that ridiculous proposal. Acceptance listening is preferable to challenge listening because it permits you to be better informed on an *entire* issue. As an informed listener, you will be in a position to make better-constructed counterproposals and gain the best agreement every time.

Your Automatic Shutoff

The automatic shutoff is a good feature in a coffeemaker or an electric iron, but it's a very bad feature in listening behavior, especially at the negotiation table. Your "automatic shutoff" is a decision to stop listening altogether. You typically do this when a portion of the negotiation involves an area in which you have little or no interest. Perhaps the other side has made a proposal so outlandish that you don't think it's even worthy of your attention. A look around any negotiation table will reveal those with their automatic shutoff engaged. Typically they avoid *all* eye contact with the presenter, and much of the time they doodle!

The problem with engaging your automatic shutoff is that it's not sufficiently selective. You are likely to miss information that is critical to other portions of the negotiation. Even if the current discussion is out of your field of specialty, you are still missing other important cues such as the strength of this part of the case as compared to others. Being on automatic shutoff prevents you from spotting flaws in the positions being presented that you might apply to your own portion of the case. Even if you're the budget person and they are discussing packaging color, there is always information to gather to be used in a "Give-to-Get" move (see Chapter 8). Engaging your automatic shutoff is a mistake no negotiator can afford.

Minimizing Distraction: Internal Obstacles to Listening

Look Forward—Not Back

It's been said that those who don't learn from history are doomed to repeat it. In negotiation, those who are too preoccupied with the past will be immobilized by it. A major source of internal distraction is the kind of looking back a negotiator does to a past part of the negotiation even as the discussion has progressed to a new issue. For example, if the other side gains a significant concession, you may feel the need to retaliate. It's possible that one of the members of the other team angered you by pointing out a flaw in your team's position—a flaw for which *you* were largely responsible. While harboring such feelings as anger or resentment may be normal or even appropriate, being preoccupied with such thoughts only impedes your ability to listen and thus your ability to negotiate.

The game of baseball provides us with a good example of the perils of looking back. Consider the role of the relief pitcher. He comes into the game to solve a problem caused by the failure of the starting pitcher. The bases may be loaded and the relief pitcher may even give up a hit. The key to dealing with the pressure is to stay focused and treat each batter he faces as an individual situation. The pitcher who looks back at what might have happened and gets rattled by the past doesn't survive.

As a negotiator, you face a situation similar to that of the relief pitcher. You must operate in the presence of a disagreement. If you look back, in the sense of being angry or frustrated about a prior portion of the negotiation, your listening skills are diminished. Similarly, the relief pitcher must treat each batter as a discrete event to ensure success. The negotiator who treats each issue or each portion of the problem as a discrete event, looking forward rather than back, will achieve the better agreement. Learn from history, but don't be immobilized by it.

Choose Logic over Emotion

If there's something in this book that's easier said than done, it's telling you to be logical when you feel like letting your emotions rule! However, in negotiation, emotions cloud your ability not only to listen but also to negotiate. It's a favorite trick of attorneys to anger opposing witnesses through a series of verbal and nonverbal tactics that range from asking tough questions in a rapid-fire fashion to turning away as the witness responds. The attorney knows that when you're angry, you are more likely to say something you shouldn't have said.

Some negotiators may even deliberately attempt to irritate you. A fabled example of such behavior is embodied by the antics of Michael J. Quill. This past president of New York's Transport Workers Union was involved in a heated negotiation with then mayor John Lindsay. Whenever the mayor's name came up in the discussions or in media coverage, and Quill made sure it was often, he would refer to the mayor derisively as "Mayor Lindsley." The constant derision angered the mayor and his staffers, making the talks much more stormy than they should have been.

Ignoring or even laughing off deliberate attempts to anger you are the best response if you are to stay on your game. Bringing your emotions to the negotiation table is going to cut down on not only your ability to focus but also your ability to listen. Remember: Getting angry or letting your emotions rule or even distract you will only sidetrack the goal of all negotiations—reaching an agreement.

External Obstacles to Listening

The Surroundings

Obstacles to listening don't all start with you, the listener. If the space is uncomfortable—too hot or too cold, too cramped or too cavernous—if the negotiation space is at an airport hotel and the view of the runway is better from the conference room than it is from the control tower, you are going to be distracted. Similarly, if there is construction going on in the next room, or the local hog-calling-contest finals are being held down the hall, you are not going to be focused on the negotiations with the constancy required. Eliminate distractions that impede the listening environment *before* rather than during negotiation.

Privacy

Privacy is another factor in providing a heightened listening environment. If media access is limited, participants will be more focused on negotiation than on what they are going to say to the media. This is just one of several reasons why media blackouts or a media communication plan—adhered to by *both* sides—is a good idea.

Privacy for the negotiators also extends to limiting outsiders' access to the participants. This means setting up rules about personal as well as cell phone access during negotiations. A limitation placed on access to the negotiators not only heightens listenership in the session itself but also limits interference with momentum, another important element in successful negotiations.

Participant Placement

At any sporting event, the most expensive seats are those closest to the action. Aside from being seen in the presence of celebrities, the major benefit of these seats is that you get to focus on the game. In negotiations, your objective in determining where you sit should be similar: *Focus on the action.*

As a student, I developed a rule that I found helpful: The more difficult the material, the closer to the front of the class I sat. In negotiation, this means that you should begin seated facing the other team, rather than choosing a seat at the other end of the room near the door, where, okay, you'll get to the food first when they bring in lunch—but really, if your focus is on lunch, perhaps you shouldn't be at the table at all.

I've already pointed out that we actually retain very little of what we hear. In addition, out-listening, challenge listening, and our susceptibility to distraction don't occur in isolation but rather overlap to make matters even worse. Awareness of these barriers to listening is a first step in improving information retention.

Sharpening Your Focus

In addition to managing the perceptual and psychological barriers to effective listening, there are some specific actions you can take to improve the rate at which you retain information.

Ask Probe Questions

Probe questions, as opposed to simple yes-or-no questions, are those that illicit a detailed response. For example, whereas a yes-or-no question sounds like this: "So, what you're telling me is that there can be no movement on the issue of the length of the service contracts?" a probe question sounds like this: "We'll need a further explanation on what seems like a lack of flexibility on the length of the service contracts." This probe question, which is actually in the form of a request, requires the opposition to flesh out their position, giving you more information and a greater chance at an opportunity to respond.

With the probe question, you also give the opposition a subtle hint that there was a flaw in their position. Even if there wasn't, you may even put your opponents on the defensive. The probe question serves a double purpose of heightening your listenership and at the same time making the other side wonder whether you sense a problem or potential weak spot in their position.

Seek Repetition

If you've ever found yourself singing the lyrics to a song you don't like, you have had a personal demonstration of how repetition builds retention. Use this principle to heighten your understanding of the other side's position by requesting a repetition of that position. In so doing, you don't need to be mysterious or to indicate you may not have been listening. Instead, a request for repetition of a statement should sound like this: "This is an important issue to everyone here, so in the interest of clarity, we'd like you to restate your position on the service contract issue, particularly the portion concerning . . ."

Repeat *Their* Position

Educators will tell you that the best way to learn something is to teach it. In negotiation, there is no better way to understand the other side's position than delivering it yourself. Begin with a statement such as "Just to make sure we all understand your position, let me see if I can take us through it."

Probe questions, clarification questions, repetition, and reviewing the other team's position don't need to occur in the sequence presented. They are each ways of eliciting information and clarifying the issues being negotiated and should be used liberally throughout negotiation to heighten your retention of the positions taken by the other side.

Taking Notes You Can Use

Many of us take notes to help us remember what went on in a meeting or at a lecture. However, if you've ever gone back and looked over those notes, you may have found that their usefulness as a retention tool is highly limited. We all filter what we see, hear, and retain through our own experiences and perceptions. Distractions and the aforementioned out-listening cycle further limit the quality of the notes we take. Following are some tips on making your notes more useful so that you can retain more of the information you hear as you negotiate.

Limit What You Write

In teaching undergraduates and lecturing in seminars, I have always distributed summary outlines in an attempt to provide some uniformity in what my listeners and students will take away from my presentation. Yet, despite informing my audiences that I'll be distributing notes, there are those who scrawl madly in an attempt to create a veritable transcript. My problem with these scribes is that a certain degree of their attention must be devoted to the motor and perceptual skills involved in the act of writing. While they may end up with a near transcript, there will be no mention of vocal emphasis, emotional pauses, or even humor. Such nuances can be detected only through a degree of listenership that's impossible if you're writing down every word you hear.

Key Words, Phrases, and Questions

If you limit your notes to three forms—key words, phrases, and questions—you'll end up with a summary of the negotiation session, which will be a useful reference tool. In addition, questions can be in the form of a single word and a question mark: possible note forms include "delivery dates?" "benefit package," "401K terms need review." For those opposed to such brevity, I remind you that expressive language is a largely automatic activity. A glance at a printed word or phrase, especially if you're familiar with the topic, can lead you to utter anything from a sentence to an hour-long lecture—all from that single word or phrase.

I encourage you to use notes as a listening and retention aid, and to reinforce the importance of keeping notes brief enough to be useful, you can use the measure often applied to simplifying visual aids: the taxi-cab test. Your slides contain too much information if you leave them in a taxi and the driver, using those slides, can deliver your entire presentation. If that same cab driver finds your notes and is able to reconstruct *exactly* what took place in a negotiation session, you're taking too many notes and—as is the point of this discussion—you're not doing enough listening!

Summary

Generally we retain very little of what we hear. However, in negotiation, the failure to listen at peak levels can be very costly. Both being aware of and managing the perceptual barriers to listening decrease this risk. Limiting internal distractions such as emotional reactions and the external distractions in the environment can also dramatically heighten your ability to listen and retain information. In negotiation, this heightened listenership will go a long way toward preventing your ever having to say, "How did we ever agree to this?"

Key Thoughts and Takeaway Points

Cut through the "noise" and break down listening barriers. Barriers to listening, or "noise" (in the sense of interference), abound in any communication situation, from visual distractions ("Where did he get that ugly tie?") to psychological distractions, such as your anger with the opposition. The visual and environmental distractions are the easiest to manage. You can either change them or simply choose to ignore them (as in the case of the ugly tie).

Psychological distractions, such as your anger with the opposing team or their position, set up a listening pattern in which you are more focused on gaining confirmation of the source of you irritation than on the negotiations themselves. In this listening pattern, you might be making a mental list of the remarks or positions you find most disturbing. At this juncture you are no longer focused on the goal of any negotiation—*reaching agreement*!

The successful management of listening during negotiations means replacing the emotional reactions to the other side and their proposals with a single and all-important question: How can we reach agreement? Answering *this* question should be your entire listening goal.

PART THREE

Advanced Tactics
and Special Situations

CHAPTER EIGHT

Advanced Negotiation Tactics

AT-A-GLANCE SUMMARY
This chapter presents tactics to use once you have internalized the "negotiation mentality." It presents tactics to use in negotiation sessions when the issues are complex or the stakes are high. You can best apply these tactics once you have gained some experience as a negotiator and you have achieved a level of sophistication that enables you to use them strategically and at will as the situation requires.

Power Tactics for Handling High-Stakes Issues

This chapter presents tactics and strategies you can use to get what you want in both formal and informal negotiations. I refer to these as "advanced" tactics because, unlike the "guerrilla tactics" presented in Chapter 2, they are more applicable to complex and consequential issues. These tactics also require more practice and a knowledge of when and where they are best applied.

Some of these tactics are aggressive and will yield dramatic results. Others are more subtle and take advantage of such factors as the other side's fatigue, lack of knowledge, or even lack of belief in their own position. These advanced tactics can be used individually or in combination to give you the clear advantage as you negotiate.

Power Tactic #1: Silence

Silence is a negotiating tactic used in conjunction with others discussed in this chapter, but it's such a powerful communicative force, it deserves special consideration. Silence is powerful because people are afraid of it—so much so that our language has developed the phrase "an awkward silence." In the presence of silence, people feel the need to jump in and cover it up, just to avoid that awkward silence.

What you have at that moment is a person who's talking without thinking. In negotiations, if you can get someone to speak before they think, you stand a greater chance of getting them to say something they shouldn't have said or make a concession they shouldn't have made. This often presents a golden opportunity to get what you want—all because you had the presence of mind to say nothing.

Power Tactic #2: The Seed of Doubt

The Seed-of-Doubt tactic involves planting a doubt in the mind of your target as to whether there is going to be any agreement or deal made. When you're negotiating over a piece of merchandise, large or small, you can employ this tactic by saying "I'm really not sure I like it all that much." Follow this statement with a strategic silence. When you're negotiating a policy question in formal negotiations, begin by saying "I'm really beginning to doubt we can come to an agreement on this. We're pretty far apart." Follow this opening salvo with the same strategic silence.

In both cases, you are expressing doubt that *anything* in terms of agreement is going to happen at all. The strategic silence that follows gives the seed of doubt a moment to take root and prod your target into action. The merchant will likely try to entice you with a better price. In a formal negotiation setting, the result is likely to be at least a reassurance that things can be worked out or at best an offer meant to show some movement.

Power Tactic #3: Good Cop / Bad Cop

You've seen TV cops question a suspect: The "bad cop" says, "If you want to get out of this place in one piece, you better talk to me," while his or her partner, the "good cop," takes the let's-have-some-coffee-and-sandwiches-and-talk-this-over approach. The theory is that the suspect will tell all to the guy with the food—anything to avoid dealing with the bad cop.

The negotiation equivalent of this routine is a team of two, one of whom is agreeable, the other of whom is not. The good cop wants to do business; the bad cop doesn't, or is at least very reluctant to. The good cop thinks the offer is adequate; the bad cop thinks it stinks (and may say so in just those terms!).

The key to success in using this tactic is to plan, practice, and be able to act as a well-choreographed team. For example, in an informal negotiation situation, such as an auto showroom, one of you will like the car; the other won't. One will think it's too expensive, while the other will think it's a stretch but worth the money. One will want to shop elsewhere; the other will say you've looked enough. The object is to get the salesperson to mediate your seeming disagreement and in so doing sweeten the deal.

In larger, more formal settings, the bad cop is the team member who thinks that a certain aspect of the agreement being negotiated is unworkable and expresses this disagreement insistently and publicly. The goal in this situation is to have the opposing team unite in trying to placate the bad cop. The role of the good cop is to take a stance that says, "I think we're not that far apart, but we have to respect Jim's [the bad cop] position." In the silence that follows, the opposition may make a counteroffer, or you may wish to make a compromise gesture to move things forward.

In formal negotiations, where the outcome is important, make certain not to overdo the Good Cop / Bad Cop tactic. Don't employ it on every item, and don't have the same team member play the bad cop every time. Once the opposing team spots this tactic, its effectiveness will be severely limited as they just wait out the bad cop's behavior.

Similarly, if the same team member objects to *every* proposal, he or she will soon be considered nothing more than a Gadfly—waited out with a there-he-goes-again stare. However, if you use the Good Cop / Bad Cop tactic selectively with a rotating cast, it stays fresh and effective.

CAUTION: In both formal and informal settings, the person who plays the bad cop should avoid theatrics. Persistence and criticality are traits of the effective negotiator, but excessive negativity and obnoxious or loud behavior are not.

Power Tactic #4: The Bluff

The bluff is a central tactic in negotiation. Simply stated, it's asking for more when everyone knows you'll take less, or making a demand that has virtually no chance of being met. For example, a union representative trying to get a 6 percent raise out of management never comes to the table asking for 6 percent. In a typical labor negotiation, the union would be lucky to get 4 percent.

The reason for the bluff in negotiation is twofold. First, if you're a representative for a group or an attorney filing a suit, the bluff is a morale booster for those you represent and can provide a degree of intimidation toward your adversaries. Second, the bluff is sometimes little more than a publicity stunt meant to attract attention to the disagreement being negotiated.

The key to a successful bluff is accurately determining the opposition's "ouch point" and asking for a figure just beyond it. Especially in cases where the negotiations take place in a public setting with wide media attention, a certain amount of bluffing is to be expected. However, making an outrageous demand just for the sake of being outrageous will prove costly. For example, initially demanding a 60 percent wage increase and immediately dropping the demand to 10 percent in the first round of negotiations, and then to 5 percent, followed shortly by 3 percent, will leave both your credibility and your effectiveness shattered. Once you begin lowering your price like an ice cream vendor during a power failure, your ability to get a worthwhile agreement will melt just like the vendor's ice cream.

Power Tactic #5: The False Concession

The false concession is a demand that's placed on the table for one purpose: to be taken off. In the give-and-take of negotiation, you will have to make concessions at some point in the process. An effective anticipatory strategy is to build conditions or items into your proposal that you have no intention of gaining. For example, in negotiating a wage settlement for an employee group, you may add a demand for an extra paid holiday in another part of the proposal, which you can withdraw as a gesture toward obtaining movement on the salary increase.

With careful planning of your false concessions, you will give up nothing (i.e., something you never had and never really wanted) to gain something! For example, in purchasing an appliance, I may make a big deal about requiring a service contract (which I consider worthless) and then give it up in exchange for a lower price.

A good source of false concessions is items that *appear* to be important but don't cost you anything. Advertising is filled with them. For example, stores that sell home furnishings will often proclaim to offer "free decorating advice." Of course it's free. Without their advice, you might not buy anything. What are they going to do—sell you stuff and then tell you to get out of the store? A radio ad for a laser eye surgeon proclaimed, "The doctor performs each and every procedure himself!" leaving me to wonder who does the surgery at other places . . . the receptionist?

In selecting false concessions to include in a proposal, find items that you can do without that *seem* to be of value. For example, if your company's computer supplier offers five-year warranties or service coverage, and you typically replace the equipment every three years, taking a two-year reduction in service support looks like a concession, but you're giving away something you'll never use.

As you select your false concession items, don't be frivolous or outlandish. Sometimes these items end up as part of an agreement since the other side had no idea you would have given them up upon request. For example, in preparing an employee group for a negotiation with their management, I suggested the inclusion of a longevity bonus as a balance against the recruitment incentives being given new employees. Management's expected response to the proposed longevity bonus was that the recruitment bonus was fair and the longevity bonus was not because of the senior employees' higher compensation rate. To our surprise, the employer granted the longevity bonus without comment. Especially in choosing false concessions, be careful what you ask for— you just might get it!

Power Tactic #6: Give to Get

The Give-to-Get tactic is driven by the principle that you shouldn't give up anything without getting something in return. This strategy works best when you have the advantage. For example, if you are the exclusive supplier of an in-demand manufacturing component, you are in a position of strength. Therefore, you can raise prices or modify delivery schedules or even adjust warranty terms in your favor.

Specifically, the Give-to-Get tactic works this way: If a contractor is asking a price for a job that was more than you expected, your response would be, "I'll agree to the higher price, but only in exchange for an earlier completion date" or "Let's set two prices, the higher one if you complete work in four weeks and the lower if the job takes longer." In both cases, you haven't given without getting.

The greater your advantage, the more aggressively you can apply this tactic. For example, if you are that exclusive supplier of a manufacturing component, the Give-to-Get tactic can become "If we get you an early delivery, how much extra per unit will you pay?" The question is closed ended and says to your target, "You will be paying more, although you have some say in how much."

The most aggressive form of this tactic comes in the form of a demand version—a closed-ended statement in which you name your own terms: "We'll approve the lower price—but on one condition."

CAUTION: When you find yourself in this favorable a position, don't overdo it. Most businesses run in cycles, which means that you will be meeting these same people on the other side of the table under less advantageous circumstances in the future. As you act, give some consideration about how you'd like them to remember you when things turn to their favor.

The Give-to-Get strategy is particularly effective once the end of a negotiation session is in sight. At this point, participants become more susceptible to momentum (agreement tends to produce more agreement), the clock ("We've been here for ten hours; let's wrap things up"), and fatigue ("We've been over this four times—let's end it!"). Here is an example of a give-to-get statement that might be used late in a negotiation session: "We'd all like to get out of here, so here's what I propose to see if we can wrap things up: We'll give you guaranteed thirty-day delivery in exchange for a 10 percent increase in your minimum order. That's more than fair to everyone, and it will help end the day."

In this case, the negotiator has coupled the Give-to-Get tactic with a sales pitch about the fairness of the offer. There is also a strong hint that agreement will produce a rapid end to the proceedings. The tired negotiator is very likely to fall prey to this tactic. If you are accused of trying to rush things with this type of proposal (which you are), back off and propose a recess. Don't become defensive, because they'll be onto you when you try this again at the end of the next session!

If you find yourself on the receiving end of give-to-get statements, your response should be a refusal to link items and instead a proposal to examine each area separately. Also, toward the end of the session, beware of the temptation to rush due to your own fatigue. Use the Give-to-Get tactic, but especially late in the game, don't become its victim!

Power Tactic #7: Item Stacking

Another tactic that is best used toward the end of a negotiation session, when people want to get out of the room, is grouping negotiation items and issues together and trying to gain agreement on several items at once. The following negotiating tactic combines an item-stacking statement and a give-to-get proposal: "We'll give you guaranteed thirty-day delivery in exchange for a 10 percent increase in your minimum order. . . . While we're at it, let's agree to extend the length of this agreement by ninety days to keep all of us out of a session like this that much longer. And by the way . . . we'll be happy to work with a longer contract if we're the exclusive supplier. And everyone here will benefit."

If the people on the other side of the table have had it with negotiating for the day, you'll end up dictating the delivery terms, and getting an increase in the minimum order, a longer term of agreement, and if they're *really* tired, an exclusive contract. As you can see, item stacking can be very profitable if used toward the end of a session. However, if you find yourself listening to an item-stacking statement, propose an immediate recess. Item stacking used with rapid-fire give-to-get proposals is a strategy that causes many negotiators to say, after the session, "How did we ever agree to this?"

Power Tactic #8: The Squeeze Play

The Squeeze Play, as its name suggests, is a pressure tactic used to try to gain an agreement quickly. It's presented to the other negotiating team as a onetime opportunity to come to agreement. The Squeeze-Play tactic sounds like this: "We're very close. If you're willing to agree to limit the price increase to three percent, right here, right now, you've got a deal. Otherwise, we'll have to widen our search for a vendor. What about it?" If naming a number is to your disadvantage (i.e., you might do better), the Squeeze Play would sound like this: "We're very close here. We're willing to make a deal with a very limited increase, right here, right now, or we'll be forced to go elsewhere. What about it?"

The key words in the Squeeze Play are "we're very close" and "right here, right now." They offer the lure of an imminent agreement combined with the pressure of time. The Squeeze Play is a blatant pressure tactic and should be applied only if those on the other side of the table are susceptible to it. The conditions for the application of the Squeeze Play are as follows: (1) You are close to an agreement advantageous to your side; (2) the other negotiating team has engaged in a bit of foot-dragging and made the negotiations longer than they should be; (3) you actually *do* have alternatives to the people with whom you're negotiating. (Don't say you'll be going elsewhere unless you actually have somewhere else to go!)

Power Tactic # 9: The Exit

Another pressure tactic, the Exit, is an option when you've tried hard to arrive at an agreement and the other side won't budge; it may be time to go and wait them out. This is not to be confused with the angry departure accompanied by such words as "This whole session is a complete waste of time and we're ending it right now!"

Since negotiation is the attempt to arrive at an agreement and not an attempt to beat up the other side, an exit accompanied by an angry outburst is also an admission that the negotiations have failed completely. However, if the opposing team is stalling or totally inflexible, an exit may be in order. Keep in mind, though, that an exit should indicate that you're willing to talk further but there is no point in talking right now.

Here is some suggested exit language: "We'd like very much to arrive at an agreement, but it's just not happening. It's best you talk among yourselves and see how much better you can do on this issue. We'll leave you alone to talk things over, but we'd like to hear from you within twenty-four hours."

This statement is minimally confrontational ("see how much better you can do on this issue"). Also, note that the need for movement is given as an absolute, not a mere possibility. The exit part of the statement gives a suggested deadline and doesn't slam any doors. This way, after the passage of the deadline, your contacting them will appear not as a capitulation, but only as real interest in reaching an agreement.

In the informal or less consequential negotiation, such as dealing with a merchant, or in any onetime negotiation, a variation of the Exit is to simply hand over a business card and say, "Call me in the next day or so if you have a better offer." If the target calls back, you'll get what you want. If not, it's probably a deal from which you should have walked away.

Power Tactic #10: The What-If

The What-If is a tactic used to squeeze one more concession out of the other side. Once you are near agreement or down to a final offer, pose an additional condition and see if the other negotiating team will go for it. If you're discussing a pricing issue and have established an agreed-upon price, push things a step further by asking for an additional quantity discount. When the point of negotiation is a single item, the What-If tactic can sound like this: "What if I buy two . . . twenty . . . one-hundred?" When the point of negotiation is a deadline, this tactic sounds like this: "What if we make the delivery two days ahead of schedule?" For a salary negotiation, the What-If tactic sounds like this: "What if I can get the sales ten percent above last year's figures?"

The What-If tactic is a last-minute move that counts on a bit of surprise as well as the other negotiating team's fatigue or willingness to be rushed. Be sure not to make it a focal point or deal breaker. However, in a culture where people aren't expecting negotiation, or where even negotiation itself is a very polite affair, the opposing team's surprise at your ability to push ahead even with agreement at hand may get you just a bit extra or, at worst, a polite decline.

Power Tactic #11: Just Ask!

Amid the strategies for trying to talk your way to getting more, it is easy to forget the simplest strategy of all—asking the other side for a concession: a lower price, a better deal, or some kind of improvement over the offer on the table. From the relatively mild "Can you do better?" to the more confrontational "You've got to do better," these proposals call for the other negotiating team to do more—something they won't usually do on their own.

Using the Just-Ask tactic, I once made $5,000 in less than thirty seconds. After agreeing to buy a piece of real estate, I said to the broker, "This deal went through with very little effort for anyone, and I was wondering if you'd take that into consideration and give me a break on your commission." Without hesitation, she agreed to a $5,000 reduction. Had she said no, I still would have gone through with the deal, but this $5,000 was mine without any strategizing or fallback positions or bluffs. All I did was ask!

The better deal often goes to the superior and strategic negotiator. However, sometimes the advantage is there for the asking. The problem is, if you don't think like a negotiator, you won't even bother to ask the question!

Power Tactic #12: The Silent Fondle

I know the Silent Fondle sounds like something talked about on tabloid TV, but it's actually a bargaining tactic you can use when trying to get the best price on a purchase. Remember the "Please don't squeeze the Charmin" advertising campaign? It was cleverly based on the premise that as you walk around a store, if you pick up an item, you are more likely to drop it into your shopping cart. Similarly, if a merchant sees you pick up and examine an item, he or she is going to assume you're interested.

The Silent Fondle works this way: Pick up the item and examine it carefully. If you're with someone, have your companion engage in some additional fondling—but do so silently. Then put the item back on the shelf and look at it for a few more seconds. At this point, the merchant will often come over and attempt to fill in the awkward silence by volunteering, "If you'd like that item, I can do better on the price." Think of it: You haven't said anything, and the other side is already negotiating with you!

If you don't get any reaction to your first fondle, walk around the store, come back to that item, and begin the fondling game once more. Even if the merchant then makes you an acceptable offer, in the spirit of a true negotiator, you'll use it as a starting point for further negotiation.

The Silent Fondle works even with big-ticket items such as cars and houses. Of course, with larger items the fondle must become an ogle. Look over every inch of the car or the house or the piece of land, but do so in silence. Let the target guess what your impressions are. Use the silence to get information with which to bargain. During such silences, I've had salespersons say things like "They've had a tough time selling this place," or "They'd be willing to replace the floors if that will help," or "That car has been sitting here a while, and I'm sure we could make a great deal!"

In each instance, you have said nothing, and, in so doing, you've gotten the other side to take a position. If the other party is under pressure to sell, your silence will only bring an expression of that pressure or information you can use when you begin to bargain. In fact, once the other party has ventured an offer, more important than the offer is the fact that he or she has opened the door to *more* negotiation.

Power Tactic #13: Devaluing the Item

Another approach to getting the best price is to make some kind of remark indicating that you don't think too highly of the item in question, and then go on to one of the strategies discussed previously. If you make a devaluing remark, keep it real. There are those negotiators who would try to devalue the *Mona Lisa* by saying, "I like the painting, but that smile kind of kills it for me." Pick a flaw and point it out, or state that you are less than very interested in an item, except at the right price.

Here are some sample devaluing statements:

1. "I don't really have much use for this—how much of a discount can I get on it?" While the statement is polite, it sill discourages a yes-no response in favor of a numerical answer.

2. "Has this been repaired? Is that water damage? What's that smell?" The neat thing about questions such as these or a reference to the tiniest flaw in an item is that sometimes you end up with an admission you weren't expecting, for example, "You're the first person to notice the smoke damage." Admission or not, you've devalued the item in the mind of the seller. Having done so, go right to "How much of a discount can I get?"

3. "I know my wife [husband, partner] will hate this thing. How much of break can you give me on it?" I call this the "marriage discount." Even if you're single, you must know by

now that couples have been blaming each other throughout history for just about everything. So, if you can't devalue an item on any legitimate grounds, go ahead and drag your real or even imagined spouse into the picture. You'll not only get the vendor's sympathy; you may also get a discount!

Power Tactic #14: The *Bajour*

The *Bajour* is actually a strategy I am advising you *against* using. *Bajour* is a gypsy term for a big score or swindle, as well as the name of a Broadway musical of several decades past.

Sometimes in negotiation you'll come upon an opportunity to make that big score, that deal that's all too lopsided in your favor—usually because the person on the other end of the deal is new at negotiation or somehow ill informed. For example, if a new buyer is about to pay too much for an order because he or she is expecting a gross of an item but has ordered only a dozen, you have a momentary advantage, at least until that order is shipped and the error is discovered. Maybe there is a misplaced decimal point or a zero on a contract that means you'll gain an advantage you shouldn't.

Enjoy your short-lived triumph. But remember the next time you meet that ill-informed dupe, he or she will have learned from the mistake, and instead of a negotiating partner, you'll encounter two huge obstacles—an enemy and a bad reputation. Sure, negotiate consistently and vigorously, but do so honestly, and the many good deals and agreements you make will far outweigh that one *bajour*.

How Do You Find Their Ouch Point?

The expected give-and-take of negotiation requires that you ask for more than you expect, but the ultimate purpose of negotiation is agreement. Therefore, going too far with a bluff can work against you. The resolution of this conflict lies in making your bluff exceed the other side's "ouch point," but not by too far. Based on my experience as a negotiator, I have developed the 30 percent rule.

The 30 Percent Rule

Simply stated, a good guideline in numerical negotiation is to ask for 30 percent more than you expect and work down to your lowest number in two but no more than three fallback positions. Using 30 percent as a guide for your initial offer will usually get you near the other side's ouch point without diminishing your credibility.

Here's how to apply the 30 percent rule: If you are negotiating for a wage increase and seeking 15 percent, ask for 20 percent and, if necessary, reduce your request to 15 percent in two steps.

Your particular situation may necessitate that you raise or lower the 30 percent figure slightly, but be careful. When numbers get above 30 percent of expectations, be it in a wage demand, a discount on merchandise, or the rapid collapse of a deadline ("We'll deliver the goods in three days instead of thirty"), it's usually because something is wrong. Either someone hasn't been telling the truth, someone has made a miscalculation, or the negotiator is simply desperate. No matter what the reason, you should find out more before making an agreement with these people! Think about how often you've seen an ad that said, "50 Percent Off!" in large print followed by an asterisk directing you to some small print the seller hopes you won't read. The fact is that in any negotiation, when a set of numbers is more than 30 percent over or under what it should be, the credibility of the people behind those numbers suffers and the climate in which an agreement can be reached deteriorates. Even in a bluff, don't stray too far beyond the 30 percent guideline.

Fallback Positions

Since negotiation is a matter of offer versus counteroffer, your first position is likely to be seen as just that, a first and not a final offer. My recommendation for the number of fallback positions you should have is two, with an absolute maximum of three. Multiple and seemingly limitless fallback positions will only convince those sitting across from you that you are either stingy (dropping your demand in five 1 percent increments) or desperate (three 10 percent increments). In either case, your game of numerical charades will prove costly in the final agreement. Limit your fallback positions to two or a maximum of three, with each position having a firm rationale. Since this is a negotiation, you should attempt to gain a concession each time you go to a fallback position (see "Power Tactic #6: Give to Get").

Plan your initial offer and fallback positions before you begin negotiations, with the final position being your real and *absolute* minimum or that beyond which you cannot do business. If your numbers have some basis in reality, they are very likely to be accepted by the other side.

Risk versus Reward

Negotiation strategies, like investments, carry risk-benefit ratios. Just as the aggressive investor seeks lofty returns, with a chance of significant losses, the aggressive negotiator has a similar risk-reward pattern. Therefore, you should examine the risks and rewards of any negotiation—what you will gain if you succeed and what you will lose if you don't. Also, in assessing risks, when you are about to make an aggressive or confrontational move, make sure you have somewhere else to go—another place, another supplier, or an opportunity to begin again should your initial efforts not produce the outcome you were seeking. Additionally, having a real backup plan gives you the power to negotiate even harder, turning that greater risk into an even greater reward!

Summary

The key to using the information in this chapter successfully is *total* familiarity with these tactics and strategies to the extent that you can use them in isolation or in sequence with seeming spontaneity. Review this chapter often and become familiar enough with its contents that a glance at a heading or tactic name permits you to construct a scenario to which it can be applied. Once you have internalized this information, you will also have gained an ability to apply it at will to a wide array of situations and negotiation problems and gain the advantage.

But remember: Negotiation is more than strategies and tactics. It is also about interaction with people. In applying these tactics and strategies, you will also develop an awareness of what works best for you and your interpersonal style. Once achieved, this level of self-awareness and tactical knowledge is a combination that ensures that you're becoming a powerful and accomplished negotiator!

Key Thoughts and Takeaway Points

Behold the power of silence! The phrase "an awkward silence," along with the notion that since talking is success, silence is failure, has made the strategic use of silence a lost art. Instead of fearing it, use silence to your advantage. When it's your turn to speak, respond after a pause of a few seconds. If the other side has just made a proposal or stated a position that's somewhat outlandish or was a bluff, your silence will turn into a moment for them to back away from the position they have just taken. Anytime your silence is punctuated by the other side's saying "Okay, I guess we can do better," you've gained an advantage by saying nothing!

Just ask! Especially when you've been reading about tactics and strategies, you might be lulled into ignoring the obvious, so it's worth a mention at this point: The beginning of many negotiations can simply take the form of asking for a better price, longer terms, a lower interest rate, and so on. Once you know there is some flexibility, *then* bring on the tactics!

CHAPTER NINE

Negotiation Countermeasures

AT-A-GLANCE SUMMARY
This chapter is about what to do when you're on the receiving end of many of the strategies and tactics already discussed. Negotiation tactics and ploys are easy to spot once you've been their victim. This chapter changes that picture by showing you how to think and act quickly to neutralize the strategies and tactics of the other side and make sure that you're playing on a level field at all times.

Better to Give than to Receive

The biblical notion that it is better to give than to receive is especially true if you find yourself the target of the strategies and tactics presented in prior chapters. I can't guarantee that you won't come across a negotiator who has read this book and is skilled in using the information presented in it. This chapter presents a series of countermeasures to enable you to effectively parry the other side's negotiating tactics as they attempt to gain the upper hand.

Strategies and Their Countermeasures

The Ultimatum

"This situation [service, price, deadline] is completely unacceptable."

The statement of the problem in the Ultimatum is followed by a deliberate and strategic silence, accompanied, if the negotiator is really on his or her game, by a piercing glare. The intent here is to put you on the defensive. The silence is added in the hope that you will attempt to break it by saying something you shouldn't say, hopefully (from their point of view) in the form of a hasty concession.

COUNTERMEASURE: Defuse and Dismiss

The Ultimatum is effectively countered by defusing the situation and breaking the silence without making an offer; for example, "Mr. Collins, I'm really sorry you feel that way, but there's really nothing I can do to change things." Follow this statement with your own strategic silence.

The goal in employing this countermeasure is *not* to make a concession. You may have a fallback position (a concession), but it's best not to go to it right away since an immediate concession is likely only to embolden the negotiator. Once you employ this countermeasure, be prepared for some verbal pyrotechnics. While you have offered an apology, you have also refused to budge. In response to the barrage that may follow, simply repeat your defuse-and-dismiss statement and remember that the one who talks the loudest in these exchanges loses the advantage.

Bonus Tip

Be certain to use the negotiator's name in your response, using a first name only with permission ("May I call you Bill?"). Anonymity enables a greater degree of confrontation, while the familiarity suggested by the use of a name softens the encounter—a good tactic when you have to deliver some bad news.

CAUTION: In delivering your response, avoid such language as "I'd really like to make an exception, but we just can't because . . ." In the pressure of the moment, you are admitting the weakness of your position and separating yourself from the organization, as if to say to the other negotiator, "You're right; it's this stupid company I work for." In effect, you are agreeing with the negotiator, which will only cause him or her to persist. Instead, keep it brief and impersonal. *Defuse and dismiss!*

The Ultimatum Plus

"These numbers are totally unacceptable. I'll do with nothing less than a fifty percent cut in the price and an earlier delivery date."

Your response to an ultimatum accompanied by a specific demand depends on your position. If you have a counteroffer to make, this is the time to make it, but do so deliberately and calmly or after a recess, so as not to appear to be yielding to the pressure of the moment. If you are going to stand your ground, here is how to do it:

COUNTERMEASURE: Respond, Stand, and Repeat
"I am really sorry you feel that way, Mr. Garcia, but your request is just not possible," or, if a concession is justified, "I'm sorry, Mr. Garcia, but the very best we can do is a ten percent reduction, although the delivery rate will have to remain firm."

Of course, as is the case in resisting the pressure of any ultimatum, once you've delivered the bad news, you can expect a loud or unpleasant response. Once again, as was the case with the straight ultimatum, remember that the one who talks the loudest loses the advantage. After the barrage from the other side, quietly repeat your position and remain silent.

The Ultimatum Exit
"If we can't settle this, right now, we're leaving!

COUNTERMEASURE: Let Them Walk!
The Ultimatum Exit is a pressure tactic that may be aimed more at the media or the other side's constituents than it is at you. If it's appropriate to the issue and the climate, you may venture a hope that the talks can be resumed, but if the other negotiating team is threatening to exit, they've probably already decided to do so. If the Ultimatum Exit works once, they'll try it again. It's a pressure tactic you shouldn't submit to, or it will be the other team's response to *every* perceived impasse.

Research and Destroy
"We both know Axle Motors is selling the same vehicle for $2,000 less. If you want this sale, you have to do better."

COUNTERMEASURE: Informational Counterpunch

This tactic refers to the other side's destroying your position with facts, a tactical application of the maxim "Knowledge is power." The best counterpunch for this is your knowledge of the other party's position. Your response would sound like this: "On the surface, your information may be correct, but if you really look at the facts . . ."

You can also disarm the other side by agreeing and countering with what is known as the "Yes, but . . ." tactic. Agree, but quickly follow up with your version of their facts. "Yes, but if you look at the deal more closely, you'll find it isn't exactly the same. For example, if you have a problem with a product of theirs, they give you an 800 number to call. If you need service from us, call me and I'll make sure it gets done." (Note that what's being offered here is an intangible that won't add to the cost of the deal.) Fight facts with more facts.

Goodwill Hunting

"It's good to be dealing with someone with your level of experience. A lot of the people I meet don't know their products at all."

COUNTERMEASURE: Thank Them and Get Back to Business

While you may anticipate the tough situations you face, most of us don't expect a compliment from an unlikely source and therefore feel the need to return the compliment. In negotiation, the giver of the compliment is seeking some form of preferential treatment or concession. As the recipient of the compliment, say thanks and get back to business! The key to not being lulled into a concession in these situations is to treat the compliment and the business transaction as totally discrete events, even as the negotiator tries to link them and gain a concession. Your response might be "Thanks for those kind words, but one secret to my success is treating *every* customer fairly."

Solve a Problem
"It's a shame you're stuck with all that inventory. I have a proposal . . ."

COUNTERMEASURE: Disagree and Deny
"Stuck? I wouldn't put it that way at all! The inventory level is *exactly* where it should be for this time of year."

The negotiator is trying to present what he or she wants as a solution to your problem. By denying that there is any such problem, you simply and effectively stop this line of negotiation. Having said that, I should remind you, as in any negotiation, be truthful. If you have a problem (such as excess inventory), denying it just to gain a *minor* negotiating triumph is bad business. There is no need to throw up your hands and say "You got me!" But this might be a time to come to a mutually beneficial agreement. However, if the facts are on your side and the other party is only trying to gain an advantage by creating a problem, go ahead—*disagree and deny.*

Silence
The negotiator may deliver a strategic silence, often in conjunction with another tactic, such as the Ultimatum or the Bluff. The goal is to pressure you into being rushed and saying something you shouldn't say just to cover the silence. In negotiation, unlike in conversation, there are no awkward silences, only awkward statements!

COUNTERMEASURE: Wait, Question, and Return
"You seem as if you were going to add something" or "To which part of the issue would you like a response?"

First, by waiting for a few seconds, you demonstrate that you're not unnerved by silence. Second, by breaking the silence with a question or a comment on the silence itself ("You seem as if you were going to add something"), you put any pressure for someone to say something back on the other side of the table.

Bonus Tip

When using silence, either as a tactic or in countering silence that's being used to pressure you, use eye contact to heighten the pressure you create. Look directly at your subject as you wait for a response, or when you're its recipient, as you deliver the "Were you going to add something?" question.

The Seed of Doubt

"I'm really not sure we can come to any sort of agreement. After all, we're pretty far apart on a lot of issues"

COUNTERMEASURE: Polite Disagreement

The seed of doubt comes in the form of pessimism or discouragement and is meant to slow down the pace of negotiations or to wear you down in hopes of gaining further concessions. The antidote for this pessimism is optimism. Say, "I don't think that's the case at all. In fact, I think we've made progress on a number of issues, and . . ." In formal negotiations, any such statement of pessimism may also be a sign of fatigue, which should be the signal for a recess.

Bonus Tip

Avoid responses like "Tell me more" or "What makes you feel that way?" These replies encourage the other side to engage in negative banter which, at this point, will only invite the planting of more of seeds of doubt.

Good Cop / Bad Cop

One team member is bellicose and totally disagreeable while another says things like "We may be near agreement, but I think Jim [the bad cop] has a point."

The assumption is that the bad cop intimidates you while the good cop quietly gets you to make concessions in an effort to quiet the monster seated across the negotiating table.

COUNTERMEASURE: Verbal Inclusion / Nonverbal Exclusion
Make sure you mention the bad cop by name in your responses so that he or she is included and his or her concerns are seemingly addressed. However, never engage the bad cop directly or respond in kind to his or her outbursts. Don't comment on the bad cop's antics or emotional state. To do so is to lose control of the situation by making the negotiation about behavior instead of the point under discussion.

On the nonverbal side, make sure your eye contact in the negotiation is to the good cop and the rest of his team but *never* to the bad cop. As a further means of isolating the bad cop, if the spatial arrangement permits, turn your body and direct your remarks away from the bad cop and toward other members of the group as you respond. These tactics will neutralize the bad cop as well as discourage his or her behavior.

The Bluff
The Bluff—asking for more than you could possibly get or for a concession that borders on the outrageous—is used for three reasons: first, as an attempt to establish the authority of the negotiator making the bluff; second, as a morale booster for the team or other constituents; third, as an attempt at the it's-so-crazy-it-just-might-work school of reasoning. Once in a great while (but not often), the other side falls for it.

COUNTERMEASURE: Thanks, But No, Thanks
Since the Bluff is often more about the bluffer than about the issue, let it go. You might even thank him or her for those thoughts on the issue under negotiation; however, the "no, thanks" should be polite but firm: "Thanks for that presentation of your position, but in the same spirit of candor, I must say your proposal is just not acceptable."

CAUTION: There is nothing to be gained by attacking the integrity or seriousness of the bluffer. If he or she was just trying to establish some authority or boost team morale and you thwart that effort, the bluffer will just have to try again and waste more of everyone's time. Let him or her bluff, dismiss the proposal, and move on!

The False Concession
"If it will help, we'll add an extended warranty for a period of one year for your order."

COUNTERMEASURE: Ask Questions and Do Your Homework
For example, you might agree to the extended warranty and give a distributor an order based on that concession. If you have done your homework, you might have learned that the manufacturer was *already* extending the warranty because of problems with the product. The distributor was making a false concession—passing off something he or she got for free as something of value. In addition to doing your homework, ask a simple question such as how much that warranty extension will add to the price. And, as usual, if a concession comes too quickly or seems too good to be true, it probably is!

Give to Get
"You do better on the delivery date, and we'll do better on the price."

COUNTERMEASURE: Proceed with Caution!
As much as it is a tactic, the Give-to-Get strategy is also an essential part of the negotiating process—a kind of trading your way to agreement. The danger in the Give-to-Get tactic is at its greatest toward the end of a negotiation session, when there is often a tendency to rush to agreement.

When you hear phrases along the lines of "You give us this and we'll give you that," it's important to break the momentum with a short recess. Just as a twenty-second time-out on the basketball court can break the other team's stride, a short recess will enable you to take a closer look at just what you are giving up and *exactly* what you are gaining in return. Don't be scared off when on the receiving end of the Give-to-Get—proceed with caution!

Item Stacking

"Since we settled the salary issue, let's extend the length of the contract by six months and put a temporary freeze on the number of benefit packages, just until we give them another look. That will wrap things up nicely for both sides, and, I'm happy to add, in record time!"

COUNTERMEASURE: Just Say No

Momentum is an important component in helping negotiations proceed to agreement, and you should definitely use this tactic toward the end of any negotiation; but since we're talking about *countermeasures,* don't let yourself become a victim of item stacking. References to time ("in record time"), getting the session over with ("That will wrap things up"), and agreement ("Since we settled on") are all cues that some item stacking is about to be attempted. If you need a recess, take it, but don't be lured into making rapid-fire concessions as the item stacker will encourage you to do. If you don't slow down or say no at this juncture, you'll end up saying "Did we really agree to this?" at a later date.

The Squeeze Play

"We're very close. If you agree to limit price increases to three percent, right here, right now, you've got a deal. Otherwise, we'll have to shop around."

COUNTERMEASURE: Cool Off and Come Back

If it's really a good deal and you should take it, do so, but not in a split second. This is a particularly important time to remind yourself that negotiating is about reaching agreement. The people on the other side *may* be justified in trying to apply pressure. But even if they are, especially in an important negotiation, it's essential to be prudent and deliberate. There should be no problem with your saying "It sounds good, but we'll need to get back to you in an hour [week, month] with a decision." The phrase "with a decision" is important here because it lets the other side know that they have something to gain by waiting.

If the other side's position is legitimate, the same deal will be available within a reasonable time period. (The duration of the cooling-off period is a function of the complexity of the issue under negotiation.) The other party's failure to agree to a *reasonable* time extension should be a warning that something is wrong and the squeeze play is being used so you won't have time to examine the facts.

What If
"What if we pay cash, deliver sooner, extend the agreement—what are you willing to give in exchange?"

Countermeasure: Listen Carefully and Stall
The What-If is another pressure tactic, a variation on item stacking, and accordingly, you should proceed with caution. However, what the maker of the what-if statement may not realize is that he or she is unwittingly revealing places where there is room for movement—areas that you may want to gain some ground on in a later portion of the negotiation, now that they have been unwittingly revealed. For example, if dangling a volume discount is part of the other party's what-if, if you're paying attention, you've just learned that there is some room to negotiate on price!

Just Ask
"I was hoping you could do better on the price."

Countermeasure: Just Say No!
Sometimes amid all the strategizing, proposals, and counterproposals that comprise negotiation, the utterly simple request is forgotten. It

remains an essential in any negotiator's arsenal because, despite its stark simplicity, it can be very effective and efficient. Fortunately, when you're on the receiving end of the Just-Ask tactic it's also simple to counter. All you have to do—and you can do it politely—is just say no.

If your refusal to negotiate at this point is genuine and represents your final position, don't make things more difficult for yourself with a weak response such as "I'd really like to, but I can't" or an apology such as "I'm awfully sorry, but I can't." If you are in a position of strength, act like it and keep your refusal brief and to the point.

The Cash Flash
"I have six hundred dollars cash and . . ."

COUNTERMEASURE: A Check Would Be Fine
If your price is firm or if your prospective purchaser is making an offer you *can* refuse, either do so, take a check, or point out the location of the nearest ATM machine. The Cash Flash is a bluff, and your buyer is counting on your emotional reaction to the display of cash. As long as you let logic rule, the Cash Flash just won't work.

The Silent Fondle
The purpose of the Silent Fondle (or ogle) is to get you to negotiate without even being asked, saying, for example, "I can do better on that item if you like it." The strategic silence of the Silent Fondle is like a staring contest in which the person who speaks first has blinked.

COUNTERMEASURE: Ignore or Agree with Their Interest
The first way to combat silent fondlers is to totally ignore them. Since their game is to pressure you into negotiating against yourself, you can't lose by not saying anything. Eventually fondlers will crack and be reduced to a Just-Ask move if they intend to negotiate at all.

The other countermeasure to the Silent Fondle is to break the silence with a statement that both acknowledges the other party's interest and discourages negotiation, such as "I'm glad you like that item; it attracts a lot of attention." Your positive reaction to the fondler's behavior short-circuits his or her intention of pressuring you into negotiation.

Devaluing the Item

"It seems in rather rough shape. I don't know if I'm interested" or "I don't really have much use for this."

These attempts to lure you into negotiating are just that: *attempts.* In all negotiations, a key to success is knowing the issues, or in this case, the item in question. It's been my experience that item devaluers will resort to anything from dishonesty to outright insults in pursuit of their negotiation goals.

COUNTERMEASURE: Fight Negatives with Positives

For example, an automobile can be in showroom condition and the devaluer will explain away the perfect specimen by saying "It's obviously been in an accident." Remember that the devaluer is just fishing for negatives, real or imagined, that will give him or her a hook with which to negotiate. As the devaluer goes after negatives, consistently point out positives.

If the devaluer has a point or happens upon an actual negative, you should use what is known as a "Yes, but . . ." response. In the case of the car, "Yes, the mileage is high, but, as you can see from the complete maintenance records, the car is in excellent shape." Fight negatives with positives!

The *Bajour*

"There will never be an opportunity like this!" or "Okay, we'll knock seventy-five percent off our asking price—but only if you sign right now!"

When you hear statements like these, don't look at them as opportunities or concessions; look at them as warnings! They are often the ploy of an anxious negotiator trying to get you to make a deal before you know too much. In the case of the *Bajour* (big swindle) it's *essential* to the swindler that you make an agreement before you know too much.

COUNTERMEASURE: The Cooling-Off Period

Just tell the other party you need a bit more time. If any negotiation takes place, let it be about the length of the cooling-off period, not about whether you are willing to sign on the dotted line. In many legal jurisdictions, certain kinds of formal agreements have built-in cooling-off periods as a matter of law. Legitimate negotiators with legitimate offers will welcome these provisions once they know agreement is near. People with something to hide will run for the hills. Let them go—you'll be glad you did.

Summary

Once you've developed a keen awareness of the negotiation strategies at your disposal, use that same awareness to be aware that you can also be on the receiving end of negotiating tactics. This recognition, along with the countermeasures described in this chapter, will preserve your advantage from both an offensive and defensive point of view.

Key Thoughts and Takeaway Points

Deny, deny, deny! The bottom line in all countermeasures is to simply deny or dismiss the strategy or tactic being aimed at you. But in so doing, make sure your turning them down is polite and to the point. For example, if you are the recipient of an ultimatum, a sympathetically delivered response that amounts to "There is nothing I can do about it" effectively neutralizes the use of the tactic.

Internalize the strategies. The negotiator who can spot such tactics as Item Stacking or Devaluing can respond most effectively. Getting a hit in baseball means getting just the pitch you want. If you can anticipate the pitch that's coming, you can put one over the left-field fence. Similarly, in negotiation, as you recognize the other party's tactic, you can use the countermeasure to neutralize the opposition's game plan.

CHAPTER TEN

Cross-Cultural Negotiations

AT-A-GLANCE SUMMARY
This chapter is about how to handle negotiations that take place outside your own culture. Ethnocentricity, differences in how you view relationships, authority, and even time can cause negotiations to fail despite your best efforts. In this chapter you'll learn to anticipate and understand how different cultural perspectives can alter the pace and progress of negotiations. You'll also learn how to work with and through those differences on the way to the common goal of agreement.

Negotiating across Borders

Aside from the usual markers of one's culture—such elements as history, language, music, dress, cuisine—the way you interact with others also defines and characterizes your culture. In cross-cultural negotiation, an understanding of the differences you encounter in interpersonal behaviors is essential to success.

When you are negotiating within your own culture, the set of interpersonal rules by which you operate—for example, how directly or indirectly you handle conflict—is very much like electricity; you hardly notice it until it's not there. As a negotiator doing business in another culture, you may experience a kind of psychological power failure in that the usual negotiation behaviors and strategies either backfire completely or just aren't as effective in getting you what you want. This chapter is about getting that power turned back on—telling you what you need to know to overcome the obstacles inherent in negotiating across borders and cultures.

The Ethnocentricity Factor

Ethnocentricity is an innate feeling of self-esteem about one's culture. Within every culture, there exists a mentality that says, "Our culture works." An often present and unfortunate by-product of ethnocentrism is the idea that says, "Your culture doesn't work as well as mine!" Ethnocentrism is a kind of cultural self-preservation mechanism, but outside your native culture, keeping it in check is essential. When negotiating with members of another culture, along with the normal high regard for your own, give equal billing to the notion that their culture also works. Whatever your expectations as you negotiate across borders, don't rely on cultural differences just fading away, even if your counterparts are experienced at doing business in your culture.

The Scorpion and the Frog

The fable of the scorpion and the frog illustrates the danger of not being attentive to cultural differences, even if they are less than apparent:

One day the scorpion found himself on the bank of a river, and since he couldn't swim, he had no way to get across. Along came a frog, and the scorpion asked if he could hitch a ride across the stream on the frog's back. The frog firmly refused, saying, "You're a scorpion and you'll sting me if I let you on my back!" The scorpion dismissed the frog's concern as folly, pointing out that they would *both* drown if any stinging went on. Convinced of his safety, the frog relented and the scorpion hopped up on his back. Midway through their brief voyage, the scorpion stung the frog and they both began to drown. Bewildered, the frog cried out, "How could you sting me? Now we are both going to die!" Said the scorpion, "I can't help it. It's my nature."

The negotiator who ignores the differences between cultures, just like the frog, is sure to get stung. In cross-cultural negotiations, ethnocentrism can heighten the extent to which negotiators cling to their ways of communicating. Often mere recognition and an understanding of the different paths to reaching the same conclusion will result in an earlier and successful outcome.

Managing Cultural Differences

The major cultural differences that affect successful negotiation include collectivist versus individualist approaches, direct versus indirect styles of communication, perceptions of time, and approaches to conflict management. This section presents strategies that facilitate successful negotiation in the presence of these differences.

Collectivist versus Individualist Cultures

In some cultures, individual achievement is valued over the good of many. In other cultures, the work of the individual is valued less than what he or she can contribute to the organization or the society. Sociologists refer to these different approaches as *collectivist* cultures and *individualist* cultures.

For example, the American culture is individualist, while the Japanese culture is collectivist. The differences between the types of social systems are apparent in daily life. To see these differences in action, one need only compare the Tokyo and New York subways at rush hour. In New York, commuters pile into a crowded subway car, yet, even on the most crowded train, passengers have their own "space." As crowded as it gets, passengers almost never actually touch or lean against each other. Violators of this rule will elicit the sharpest of stares.

In Tokyo at the height of rush hour, conductors on the platform literally pack people into the trains until every square inch of space is taken. Even on a subway train, the common good—that *everyone* gets to their destination as soon as possible—is more important than individual comfort. Personal space is sacrificed for the common good.

Collectivist versus individualist outlooks have profound effects at the negotiation table and can lead to serious friction and disruption of the process if not recognized. For example, the member of an individualist culture is more likely to seek personal victory at the negotiating table, while the collectivist negotiator will work toward the good of his or her team. The individual negotiator is likely to push for movement and change right there at the negotiating table in the spirit of individual accomplishment. The collectivist has little interest in pushing ahead but is more interested in the broad or collectivist effects of the agreements being made. Thus, in the presence of the individualist negotiator (e.g., an American), the collectivist negotiator will seem hesitant, unyielding, and overly consultative. If the individualist negotiator fails to take heed of the cultural difference in operation and pushes harder out of frustration, he or she will only drive the collectivist negotiator further away from agreement. Neither approach is better; they're just different.

Research has shown that members of Western cultures, including the United States, Scandinavia, Europe, and Australia, tend to take the individualist approach to negotiation. In contrast, people from a far-flung array of places including the Pacific Rim, Turkey, Greece, and Pakistan, to name just a few, are likely to favor a more collectivist approach.[*] While such generalizations might be interesting and provide a guide as to your expectations, they can also be shattered by the education, experience, and the internationality of the other team.

Negotiating in the Collectivist Culture

Since the goal of negotiation is agreement, not victory, being an individualist negotiating in a collectivist culture means recognizing the fundamental difference in the approach to problem solving. For example, if the other negotiating team takes frequent recesses to go off and huddle in order to formulate a position, recognize that it's the collectivist way of doing business. Not acknowledging this behavior as a culturally based difference just breeds frustration on the part of the member of the individualist culture. That frustration leads to anger, and that to a vicious cycle of battles and sticking points, which if unchecked will disrupt the process entirely.

---

[*]Harry C. Triandis. *Individualism and Collectivism* (Boulder, Colorado: Westview Press, 1995).

Collectivist versus Individualist Language Strategy

Language sets and maintains the tone of any negotiation session, and the tendency of individualist negotiators to speak for *themselves* contrasted with the tendency of collectivist members to speak for *their team* or organization can add a further level of conflict. While language usage defines the differences between cultures, it can also be used as a means of bringing the participants closer in terms of their approach to reaching agreement.

The need for *inclusive language* (see Chapter 6) is heightened in the presence of collectivist negotiators. Getting the sides closer to agreement means making a linguistic shift toward inclusive language, with such phrases as, "Everyone here," "All of us,"and "Both teams." Similarly, proposed solutions should be presented in terms of how they will benefit the other organization as a whole rather than merely those present.

The individualist should avoid such phrases as "Here are settlement terms we can both live with" in favor of such phrases as "I know you'll want to take a closer look at these terms, but in presenting them it should be emphasized that they represent the possibility of a considerable benefit for your organization."

Presenting the terms of a proposal in language that communicates the possibility of a benefit to the organization, from the *collectivist* rather than the *individualist* point of view, makes agreement more attractive to the collectivist negotiator.

Since the collectivist negotiator is also more likely to behave in a hierarchical manner (consulting with higher-ups before coming to a decision), you will heighten that negotiator's comfort by presenting proposals with alternatives from which to choose rather than a flat position. For example, if you are negotiating a delivery date, offer several possibilities. The differences among the choices you offer may be of little or no consequence to you but will be seen as facilitating the collectivist approach toward negotiation—a momentum builder that will serve you well when it comes to negotiating more difficult items.

How to Handle the Indirect Negotiator

From a communications or negotiations perspective, the indirect culture is characterized by a gentility of expression that sets aside direct criticism or blame. For example, as a member of a culture that uses a direct style of expression, you might say, "I missed my flight." The member of a culture that favors indirect expression would express that same transportation mishap as "The plane left without me."

Indirect communication is used to soften the impact of information, preserve or maintain a state of harmony, and avoid the loss of status, or "face," a trait often ascribed to Asian cultures. Although the American culture is seen as direct when compared with others, indirect communication is, at times, alive and well. For example, in the largely social activity of dining in a restaurant, the delivery of the check at the end of the meal is done in a very indirect and apologetic manner. In the lowliest coffee shop the server routinely places the check facedown on the counter. In the trendiest four-star eatery, that much larger check is presented in a leather folder so you need look at it only when ready. Payment is then placed in the folder. This little ritual says, "We're sorry that this meal has to end with the vulgarity of a financial transaction, but we'll try to make it as inconspicuous as possible."

Similarly, one's financial status in the American culture is often a closely kept secret. Paychecks are delivered to employees in sealed envelopes. Asking someone "How much do you earn?" or "How are your investments doing?" or any question that seeks to strip away the illusion of success is considered off limits. So while Americans may be direct at the negotiating table, we too have an indirect approach to certain issues.

Generalizing as to which culture takes a more direct approach to negotiation can be dangerous given the globalization brought about by the interaction of cultures through increased international travel and the accelerated degree to which information travels via the Internet. One indicator I have used in my international dealings is as follows: The degree of directness is inversely proportional to the degree of ritual social interaction that accompanies a business transaction. For example, if a negotiation session is scheduled for 9 AM and begins with coffee and everyone is seated around the table by 9:30 AM, the hosting negotiating team will expect and tolerate a direct approach. However, if the meeting is preceded by a gala dinner and a visit to a local cultural attraction the evening before the negotiation, be prepared to take an indirect approach. The level of intercultural experience of your negotiation counterparts as well as their expectations of your behavior are likely to be the ultimate determiner of how they will approach negotiation.

Structuring the Meeting

The indirect negotiator is likely to see you, the direct negotiator, as overbearing and overly aggressive and therefore will be expecting a tough session. An effective means of countering that expectation and smoothing the path toward agreement lies in giving the indirect negotiator plenty of input on the meeting structure: time, place, and number of people in the room. To the indirect negotiator, these elements will be seen as conciliatory gestures, which, under most circumstances, cost you nothing but set a positive tone for reaching agreement.

A classic example of an indirect negotiating environment was that of the Paris peace talks, held to negotiate an end to the involvement of the United States in the war in Vietnam. Feelings were strong on both sides that an end to military action was overdue. However, prior to the substantive negotiations, nearly two months were consumed deciding on everything from the shape of the table to the status and number of participants who should attend from both sides. The matter of saving face was hardly restricted to the North Vietnamese, since the United States could not claim victory after nearly a decade of fighting. The result was as much negotiation about the negotiations as there was about the military conflict.

In negotiations with cultures preferring the indirect approach, there is certainly no harm in making the meeting structure, schedule, or environment elements to be conceded with little or no resistance. These concessions are not costly in the long run, whereas they provide a degree of momentum that will be helpful as you proceed toward more central issues.

Pose Questions Instead of Taking Positions

The negotiator from a so-called direct culture is expecting a give-and-take in negotiations. The indirect negotiator's version of give-and-take is "receive, then let me think about this for a while, check with my superiors, and then get back to you." As a negotiator, you will get further facilitating this cultural difference rather than bumping up against and becoming exasperated by it.

Movement with the indirect negotiator will come more slowly than it would with another direct negotiator, but it will come if the negotiation activity is viewed and constructed as a journey with a series of stops rather than a battle from which the indirect negotiator will withdraw if the fighting is too intense. Battle is avoided with such questions as "How do you think we can get closer on the issue of wages?" rather than "These numbers are completely unacceptable! You'll have to do better." Such a blunt statement is likely to send your counterparts into a retreat, during which, rather than trying to come up with new numbers, they will be looking for someone else with whom to do business.

Time as a Cultural Variable

The way members of a culture view time impacts the way they negotiate. Being unaware of or inattentive to how members of a culture view time or the rate at which they prefer to negotiate can make the process *seem* much more difficult.

In many Western cultures, time is viewed as a valuable commodity. Adherence to strict schedules is seen as a virtue and the inability or lack of desire to do so a flaw. For example, KLM Airlines for many years referred to itself as the airline run by "the careful, punctual Dutch." Federal Express brandishes the slogan "The world on time." The American business culture runs on the phrase "Time is money. " Other cultures view time as a less crucial element in the game.

A contrasting view of time, as something to be spent rather than saved, can be seen in the way dental treatment is handled in a Latin American country as compared to many Western cultures. For example, in America if you need to see a dentist immediately, your dentist's office is very likely to tell you, "We can squeeze you in at twelve thirty." In other cultures, this exchange might go quite differently. For example, a friend of mine had a dental emergency on a visit to Latin America. He was delighted by the come-over-right-away response from the receptionist. Upon arriving, he was surprised to see a packed waiting room in which he spent more than an hour waiting to see the dentist. After being treated, he asked the receptionist about the appointment process. Her response? "We just open in the morning and see patients as they come in. If we made appointments, no one would keep them."

As a negotiator operating in a culture where time is not considered a valuable commodity, or is viewed differently from time in Western cultures, be prepared to adjust. Late or leisurely starts are likely to be taken by the member of a more time-intense culture as snubs or tactical attempts to irritate. Being attentive to and tolerant of such differences in how people value time will go a long way in gaining acceptance as a negotiating partner.

The Value of Relationships

Another facet of how time is viewed may involve the need to spend some time socializing with your counterparts. They know that as a member of a time-intense culture you may not relish the idea of spending nonbusiness hours socializing. Therefore, your willingness to do so is an important gesture that will facilitate your negotiation efforts—all because you gave as much consideration to spending time as you usually do to saving it!

While time may be money in the American culture, relationships are equally valued in other cultures. That is to say, in people-centered cultures such as those of Asia, South America, and the Middle East, your counterparts place a high value on knowing you on some non-business level before they negotiate or do business with you. I'm not suggesting that their children will marry your children or that lifelong relationships are being formed. However, your spending time with them away from the negotiating table at least suggests a willingness to take the time to know them and their world. Within one's own culture or across borders, people still prefer negotiating and doing business with people they know.

Accordingly, pay close attention to such cues as requests that you arrive a day or two early or simple questions as to when you'll be leaving. "Did you have a preference?" is a much more astute answer to the question "When will you be leaving?" than a direct delivery of information about your flight time. Your intention to catch an early flight home and skip a farewell dinner held in your honor will also mean that you can probably say farewell to doing business with these people in the future.

A question central to any business relationship, in negotiation and beyond, is "How will these people behave in the event of a problem or unforeseen difficulty?" Behavior that says to the relationship-oriented business prospect, "I don't care to know you but I'll be delighted to do business with you," will lose you the opportunity for business well before the negotiation stage.

Recognize; Don't Patronize

When operating in a culture other than your own, it's a gesture of respect to adhere to some extent to local customs. For example, at business dinners in Asia, I have always made it a practice to use chopsticks, although I've been offered Western culinary implements at nearly every meal. I've also noticed that upon my declining the knife and fork, the conversations are warmer and the comfort level of my hosts' increases.

However, I avoid anything other than the most global commentary on political matters and even that haltingly because such comments always end up in the realm of "I feel your pain and I know what you're going through." The fact is, you haven't shared their experience and couldn't possibly know how they feel. Besides, unless you have an intimate awareness of the other culture, you run the risk of saying something really stupid.

A physician I met at a conference, a native of India, told me of his encounter with a real estate agent in the southwestern United States. Upon learning of the doctor's ethnicity, in a terribly misplaced effort at saying something ingratiating, the realtor ventured, "I'm really sorry the government took your land and put your people on reservations." Sometimes it's just better to stick to business. If you feel the need to make cross-cultural conversation, ask questions instead of making comments like that bumbling real estate agent.

Cross-Cultural Confrontation

Since most negotiation happens in the presence of disagreement, the strength and tone of that disagreement is an important variable across cultures. In direct, noncollectivist cultures, vigorous (read that as loud) disagreement is permissible and even expected. I'd caution those of you who have a tendency to get loud that my prior rule (the one who talks the loudest loses) still applies. Once you increase the decibel level either because you think those sitting across from you will respond to it or out of sheer emotion, be sure to begin with the words "It's nothing personal but . . ." And for good measure, your final words should be "But once again, it's nothing personal."

However, remember that in both collectivist and indirect cultures, confrontation will fail miserably, and increasing the decibel level will be seen as disrespectful. No amount of saying "It's nothing personal" will work in the collectivist setting. In these settings, it's always personal.

Instead of confronting, pose questions. Instead of being personal, talk about the issue, not the opposing team—about it, not them. "I have a real problem with your delivery date" becomes "The delivery date is problematic; perhaps there is an alternative. Here are some alternative dates that would be helpful in reaching agreement." By staying indirect and impersonal, you avoid having your opponent lose face. Note that in this scenario, you have provided alternatives, possibilities as far as alternate delivery dates. In this manner, you have presented a balanced situation in which you present solutions but the other side is given the option of making a decision.

Don't be irritated if the response comes in the form of a set of alternate delivery dates from which you then get to make a choice. It is simply a variation of the two polite negotiators entering the room and saying "After you." "No, after you." Amid this ritual politeness, there is agreement. You make the choices; they make the decision.

Summary

When negotiating across borders, remember the fable of the scorpion and the frog. Be it an indirect, a collectivist, or a hierarchical outlook that sends them scurrying out of the room to deliberate when you want to press ahead, remember: It's their nature. You know you're not going to change it, but by anticipating, recognizing, and even facilitating these differences, you will be better able to negotiate a successful outcome.

The behavioral expectations you have of one another are likely to result in adjustments and accommodations on both sides. Be attentive to differences in how time is viewed and the value of relationships. Pay close attention to invitations and social events. Your participation may be an important symbolic communication in terms of your worthiness as a negotiating and business partner.

Key Thoughts and Takeaway Points

Knowledge is power. This time-tested maxim is especially true when it comes to negotiating within or with members of another culture. Knowing, anticipating, and adjusting for the differences between you and your negotiating partners is infinitely preferable to having to adjust for or clean up any communicative messes that were made because of a failure to recognize what may be a radically different approach to problem solving from your own.

If they stand on ceremony, you should too. Members of Western cultures tend to "get down to business" rather quickly. However, in other cultures, negotiation may be preceded by social activities such as welcome dinners and the like. Don't be dismissive of such invitations. They are often viewed as a measure of the kind of business partner you will be should an agreement or affiliation be negotiated.

A key element in the formation of business relationships in such cultures is the social activity that precedes it—an opportunity to see you as a person, not just a business associate. A further question often addressed with such activities is what kind of person you will be once the ink has dried on an agreement—how you will respond when and if problems arise. So, even if it's been a long day and an even longer flight, put aside the jet lag and attend the welcome dinner. If you don't attend to their cross-cultural ceremonial needs, they'll find someone who will.

CHAPTER ELEVEN

When Negotiations Fail

AT-A-GLANCE SUMMARY
Sometimes the goal of all negotiations, agreement, seems impossible, or the people with whom you are negotiating are disagreeable to the extent that talking with them seems pointless. This chapter poses the questions you should ask as you seek to resume failed negotiations. It also covers ways of reaching out to the other side, when a cooling-off period is a good idea, and even when and how to walk away.

Resolving Impasses

Up to now, this book has been about how to succeed in negotiation. But since the outcome of negotiation involves the wide and rather unpredictable range of human reactions to proposals and problems, no one set of behaviors or strategies will always yield the same result. Despite elaborate planning and strategizing, failure is an ever-present possibility.

In informal negotiation, this usually means an abrupt and final end to the process. Given the trivial nature of most informal negotiations, the consequences of such failure are likely to be minimal and short-lived. In formal negotiations, however, a breakdown or sudden end to the process may pose a serious problem. This chapter addresses solutions to overcoming impasses as well as suggesting when an end to negotiations is the best option.

The breakdown may take several forms. Egos or ideas may clash in a manner that provokes a fit of temper and a walkout. A much less theatrical but equally disturbing outcome may be a late-night e-mail telling you not to bother showing up for tomorrow's session. In other words, it's over. But in the immortal and overquoted words of Yogi Berra, "It ain't over till it's over." Here, then, is how to find out if it's *really* over, and, if it isn't, how to get things moving toward agreement.

Some Crucial Questions

What Do *You* Want?

When negotiations fail, some crucial questions must be answered before you attempt to resume. The first and most central of these is, What do you want? Sometimes conflict and confrontation are normal parts of the process. But amid all the noise you must also ask, If negotiations resume, what is to be gained? Will resumption mean crawling back to a situation so riddled with conflict or to an opposition so emboldened by your call to resume that their demands will be even *more* outrageous? On the matter of personal chemistry, there is the question of whether you want to negotiate with and/or do business with these people at all.

As you answer the crucial question—What do you want?—do so logically. Gather evidence to support your decision with further questions, for example, "If I don't resume, can I go elsewhere?" "If I do resume, what will it cost?" If that cost is too great, it's time to walk away.

Determining what you and your team want as well as answering the questions that follow will provide you with information on whether the process is worth continuing.

What If *They* Walk Out on You?

Any attempt to resume negotiations in the face of a walkout should not be emotionally based. Emotion is the enemy of success in negotiations. For example, if you find yourself saying things like "I'm not giving these people the satisfaction of walking away from the negotiation" or "I'm starting up just to prove that they can't get away with this!" you are acting out of emotion rather than logic. Even if an emotional reaction is appropriate, at times like this it is essential to stay focused on the goal of agreement and whether it is still possible or even worthwhile.

Who Is the Problem?

Negotiations fail for one of two reasons: people or issues. Isolate whether your negotiations have stalled because of a *people* problem or an *issues* problem. If you are dealing with a difficult person or persons, review Chapter 4 to learn specific strategies for handling the various characters you will meet at the negotiating table. Among these are the Bully, the Bluffer, the Martian, and the Gadfly, to name just a few. The task with a people problem is to isolate that character from the negotiation process and neutralize his or her behavior.

What Is the Problem?

Assuming the impasse is a *what* and not a *who,* the issue needs to be assessed in terms of whether a solution is possible. Examine the reason for the impasse. Was it *emotionally* or *logically* based? Ego-involved negotiators worry about being perceived as weak if they make too many concessions. Therefore, they begin objecting because of a misplaced need to do so rather than because of any real objection. Since they look at the negotiation setting as a battlefield rather than a place to seek agreement, they may even back out of the session in a show of bravado, no matter how misguided such a move might be.

A clue to such ego-based behavior lies in statements such as "We've already given up too much!" Your quiet directness as contrasted with displays of ego from the other side is effective in handling the emotionally based impasse. For example, try saying "We'd like to resume negotiations and will be sure to address the issues that you feel are responsible for the impasse." With this statement, you haven't given away anything. Instead, you've simply expressed a willingness to talk further. If the other side is well intentioned albeit emotional, this type of statement should be helpful in having negotiations resume.

Reaching Out and Restarting Negotiations

On the matter of breakdowns and impasses, don't always assume the other side is at fault. Perhaps they were justified in walking away. Perhaps they have other sources (such as your competitors) with whom to negotiate. Regardless of the reason, examine the cost of letting the impasse continue, and act in *your* best interests.

The Apology

A great deal is made over whether to apologize at a negotiation impasse, since it can sometimes symbolize weakness. It means saying you were wrong and they were right. If the goal of negotiation was victory, an apology would be a mistake. However, since the goal of negotiation is agreement, an apology can be a very smart negotiating tactic. If it will make you more comfortable, throw in a few weasel words, for example, "We *may* have been off base in refusing your offer and are sorry that anyone *might have been* offended. We'd like to reconvene and see if we can work through to an agreement." If the other side accepts an apology, you've won in the sense of getting what you wanted—the resumption of the negotiations.

The Underling Approach

When the impasse has emanated from a senior team member and there will be a problem of face saving, sending out a feeler via a secondary member of your team to a secondary member of their team can be effective in getting negotiations back on track. The purpose of this overture is to say that you'd like to get talking again, at least in an informal discussion to see if there is a willingness to talk further. The results of these discussions can lead to resumption of negotiations without anyone having lost face.

The Hotline Approach

Amid the ruins of failed negotiation, the hotline approach is a direct request from one team leader to another to resume talks. A call for resumption that comes from key figures in the negotiation is a powerful tool in continuing on a positive note since it ostensibly has the support and prestige of the leaders behind it. When tensions are running high, a recommendation from either leader that a preliminary meeting take place to examine the possibility of resumption is an effective bridging device in restarting negotiations. Particularly if the negotiations are crucial or have gotten very close to agreement, the hotline approach is well worth it.

The Cooling-Off Period

Negotiations can break down because of disagreement on issues that appear to be of monumental importance at the time they are discussed. When the issues climate has become overly heated, the cooling-off period is important in breaking the negative momentum and allowing negotiators to view issues from a less conflict-ridden perspective. As you call for a recess, do so with minimal reference to the fact that the situation has deteriorated. In fact, call it a recess rather than a cooling-off period. Also be certain to agree on a schedule that includes the resumption of negotiations. After a recess, you will find that the altered perspectives provided by the mere passage of time are often enough to get around that impasse.

Dividing and Conquering

In the case of an impasse resulting from a *what* and not a *who* type of issue, another means of salvaging the situation is to separate that one sticking point from the rest of the negotiations and have a subcommittee with members of both teams examine the issue. The appointment of such subcommittees (some people think calling them "task forces" gives them more clout) works very much the way time works in altering the perspective that made that particular issue so important.

Also, since negotiation involves the infinitely variable chemistry of human interaction, which may itself be responsible for the impasse, the fact that the subcommittee will have an alternate cast of characters changes that chemistry, usually for the better, since the teams are already at an impasse.

If you choose to take the subcommittee route in an attempt to overcome an impasse, remember that the weight of the subcommittee's recommendations is going to be directly proportional to the credibility and authority of the subcommittee membership. Therefore, since you are already at an impasse, don't overstrategize in structuring a subcommittee, for example, loading it with the toughest or the meekest members of your team. Instead, choose members with credibility, knowledge, and authority. These are qualities that are most likely to appeal to *both* sides as they consider the recommendations of the subcommittee.

When to Walk Away

I have already pointed out the exit as a negotiation strategy unto itself (see Chapter 2). It is an especially effective ploy when you have somewhere else to go. However, there will also be occasions in negotiations when the deal is just unacceptable; the numbers are just too low or too high; or the offer seems to good to be true (read the fine print; it probably is).

In considering whether to walk away, ask—and answer—these questions:

1. Do these people really want an agreement?
    Sometimes, for reasons you'll never know, the other negotiating team has no intention of negotiating in good faith. If the demands are too outrageous and made too loudly, if the stares and the silences are too lengthy, walk away. If they're legitimate, they'll call you back with an explanation for their behavior and an invitation to reopen negotiations.

2. Is negotiation with you a dress rehearsal for a meeting with another party with whom the *real* negotiations will take place? Anyone who has ever left a job interview at which they performed brilliantly only to find that they did not land the job

or delivered an electrifying sales presentation only to discover that someone else landed the account can tell you that sometimes the decision is made before you get to the event. Signs of this situation are severe limits on meeting time, halfhearted or ridiculous questions, and the absence of key players. Your best bet in this situation is to make a positive impression, orchestrate a polite exit, and adjust your goals downward toward there being a next time, an option that an angry exit will preclude.

3. Are you dealing with ill-informed idiots?
   The people in charge or occupying the key seats around the negotiation table are not always the sharpest tools in the shed. Even if their names are on the door, they just may not be good businesspeople. Perhaps their proposals are outrageous, are based on misinformation, or just don't make sense. Hopefully, your prior research will help you avoid all this, but if you encounter this situation and find yourself heading for an agreement you'll only regret, it's time to make an exit.

Summary

If you ask the questions posed in this chapter and the answers keep coming up to your disadvantage, the time to negotiate has passed and the time to walk away is at hand. If your attempting a restart is in your best interests, put your ego on hold in reaching out to the other side. The organizational culture is the best determiner of whether that reaching out should be a high-level affair (hotline approach) or whether the reconnection would be best accomplished through underlings. Finally, in getting things restarted, consider the apology a clever negotiating tactic rather than a sign of weakness. Remember that the goal of all negotiation is agreement—a goal which can only be reached if both sides are talking.

Key Thoughts and Takeaway Points

Are they for real? When the other team has walked away from the table or talks have broken down, the key question to ask is, "Do they really want an agreement? Was this failure just posturing by the other side, or is it time to walk away entirely?"

No agreement is preferable to a bad agreement. Agreements made under pressure or because of a need to be liked or even a fear of walking away will only result in your having to ask the question that every negotiator dreads: "How did we ever agree to this?" You agreed to it because you forgot that no agreement is preferable to a bad one!

CHAPTER TWELVE

The Ten Commandments of Negotiation

AT-A-GLANCE SUMMARY
At several points in this book I have urged you to review and internalize certain portions of the material presented. This is especially true of strategies and tactics. This chapter is presented as a kind of lightning-round review for the reader in a hurry. It covers the essentials of *Negotiate to Win!* and ends with some words of encouragement for your future negotiating efforts.

The first eleven chapters have taken you through a wide array of strategies, tips, and behaviors to help you become a powerful and effective negotiator. This chapter represents a review of the most important principles of negotiation, principles that apply as much to the casual, spur-of-the-moment encounter as to the most elaborately structured formal negotiations.

Internalizing the Principles of Negotiation

Key to the successful application of the information contained in these pages is the internalization of the tips and strategies presented to the extent that you can apply them at will. Undoubtedly you'll want to review various sections of this book to aid in that process. However, if you find yourself in need of a quick review of the *most* important principles applicable to *any* negotiation, this chapter provides it. Here, then, are ten rules you should obey on your way to becoming a powerful negotiator, the ten commandments of negotiation:

1. Thou Shalt Let the Other Side Talk First

In both formal and informal negotiations, you gain information by hearing from the other side. Are they angry or overly aggressive? Have they prepared their case well? Who are the key members of the team—the decision makers? What do *they* see as the major and minor issues? This is all information that you can use to your advantage if you know it *before* you negotiate—information that you can get from the other side if you let them speak first. In formal negotiations, you may have to give up the advantage of talking second, or at least alternate in various parts of the negotiation, but whenever you can, let *them* be the first to talk.

2. Thou Shalt Use Silence to Your Advantage

People are afraid of silence. We routinely refer to that moment when the words stop and no one has anything to say as an "awkward silence." At any such moment, people will rush to say something—anything at all—just to cover that silence. The problem is that when people blurt out anything at all, they do so without thinking. When people talk without thinking, they often say things they shouldn't have said.

Silence is an age-old weapon used by people who ask questions for a living, such as reporters, police officers, or attorneys. Typically, they ask a question, get a response, and follow the response with silence and a stare. The unwitting soul on the receiving end of the question will often scramble to cover the silence and more often than not says something he or she didn't intend to say.

The same is true in negotiation. Upon hearing the position of the other side—especially if it's a weaker part of their case—respond with silence. Five or six seconds later, you'll be listening to a negotiator who instead of negotiating is now covering a silence—and like a hapless suspect—probably saying something he or she shouldn't say, such as "Well, I guess we can do better on that delivery date."

While you'll want to use silence to your advantage, don't fall victim to their silence and begin your own verbal ramble. If you feel the need to say something, make it a question, such as "Did you need more information?"

3. Thou Shalt Prepare Your Case and Theirs

The best negotiator is the best-prepared negotiator. You can't be the best prepared unless you can look at an issue from your perspective *and theirs.*

This is as true in negotiating a multimillion-dollar labor contract as it is in making a purchase from a flea market vendor. Each side has its limits, or "ouch point." Knowing both sides of the issue will get you closest to those limits without going so far as to shut down the negotiations.

4. Thou Shalt Always Tell the Truth

No—this is not an invitation to spill your guts and give the other side more information than they should have. In fact, you may routinely "spin" issues to your advantage—for example, claiming that a certain deadline is essential—even though you have a couple of fallback positions. That kind of give-and-take is very much a part of the process. Within any organization there is also likely to exist proprietary information that should remain off-limits to the other side.

However, negotiation should consist of a fair exchange of information necessary to make an agreement with which both sides can live. A stunt such as omitting information will ultimately cost you. For example, suppose you have a chance to dump some old merchandise at a high price as part of a deal, even though you know an improved product is about to be released. The other side will eventually realize that they have been "had," to put it in the politest of terms.

In addition to the ethical lapse, the problem with arriving at a settlement based on partial or untruthful information is that you can do it only once. The next time you're across a table from these people, they'll be out to get you. In fact, in the future, they may solve the problem by never doing business with you again. So avoid the temptation to make that big score and instead tell the truth. In the long and the short run, it's the preferable way to do business and to negotiate.

5. Thou Shalt Negotiate with the Right People

I have a rule of making sure I am talking to the right person when I am making important transactions, presenting consequential information, or even making a complaint. For example, I never negotiate with someone who sits behind a window or who wears a name tag. The decision makers in any organization are in the corner office—not behind a window or counter—and they're not wearing name tags! Time spent negotiating with someone who has no authority to make a decision is time wasted. (Chapter 1 presents some strategies for getting through to those who can make things happen.)

In informal negotiations, you may have to do some work to get to the decision makers. In formal settings, the decision makers will be either at the table or in the row behind the team members at the table. In every setting, formal or informal, find out who the players are and address your remarks to them. Find out to whom you should be speaking and go right to that level—even if it's the top.

6. Thou Shalt Avoid Displaying Internal Dissension

A motorist is stopped for speeding. As the driver and the police officer begin to debate the seriousness of the offense, the driver's wife leans toward the cop and says, "Officer, you ought to know better than to argue with him when he's been drinking." That bit of internal dissension weakened the motorist's case, to say the least.

The same is true when a member of your negotiating team decides to disagree with you in front of the other team. It can be blatant, for example, "I don't think Bill really meant to quote you a number quite that high." Of course, at this moment you may shoot a glance at Bill that would shatter a plate-glass window and he may shut up, but the damage is done.

Disunity isn't always expressed in words. Nonverbal cues such as a yawn, turning away from the speaker, or deciding to clean your glasses are all certain cues to the other side that there is disagreement with your position on this issue. So make sure the members of your team are attentive and present a united front *at all times.* Air disagreements privately and tell anyone who can't follow those simple directions to play on another team.

7. Thou Shalt Avoid Fatigue

The history of aviation is littered with the stories of pilots who have flown into mountainsides and made other disastrous errors for one reason and one reason alone—they were tired! Fatigue is the enemy that can dull the sharpest of skills and the keenest of wits.

In negotiation, fatigue can also produce disasters. Those parts of an agreement that cause you to say in the aftermath, "How did we ever agree to this? . . . What were we thinking?" are the by-products of fatigue. If you were thinking at all, you were thinking about getting things over with and getting away from that conference table. Take breaks, set time limits in advance, and observe them—this way you can avoid becoming so tired that your fatigue affects your ability to function. Be certain that breaks are scheduled in advance, and make it clear when you take a break that you are reacting to the clock rather than the issue being discussed. Scheduled breaks mean that neither side will be the victim of fatigue. There is no advantage to be gained just because the opposition is tired. If they're beat—you are too!

8. Thou Shalt Not Be Rushed

A by-product of the aforementioned fatigue is a tendency to hurry the negotiation process, particularly as the discussions start to reach a conclusion, when negotiations speed up to the point that participants begin saying things like "You agree to the new delivery date and we'll cut our shipping price per unit by another ten percent." This kind of you-do-this-and-we'll-do-that rapid-fire bartering will result in the question "How did we ever agree to this?" being heard around the office in the months to come. Concessions made in haste are usually a mistake, so don't allow yourself be rushed.

Also, as will be the case when you are negotiating a complex agreement, if you have to refer to a document and read or interpret it, do so without regard to the fact that you are interrupting the flow of the negotiations. This is a good time to take a recess and examine the material in private, but don't rush at a time like this. You'll only regret it later.

9. Thou Shalt Strive to Speak Softly

It's been my experience that in negotiations, the one who speaks the loudest loses. If you try to match the decibel level of a bully, your behavior is being controlled by that bully. Instead, remain soft-spoken and stay in control. The loud talkers will look all the more inappropriate and you'll take the best position a negotiator can have—command of the session.

10. Thou Shalt Seek Agreement, Not Victory!

"Victory isn't everything.... It's the only thing." These words were spoken by a great football coach, not a great negotiator. Football players may seek to annihilate the other side, but football is confrontation—not negotiation. In negotiation, each side seeks a way out of a disagreement, and there is an exchange of concessions to obliterate or at least diminish the level of disagreement. In negotiations, if either side receives a trouncing, there will inevitably be calls for a rematch—a repeat of the battle. That's why, after long and difficult negotiations, you are most likely to hear each side say, "We believe we achieved a fair agreement [or an agreement from which both sides will benefit]."

Each side is seated at the table because they have a degree of power or influence over the other. The fact that you are both there suggests a certain balance of power that neither side is going to relinquish. So, despite the threats, histrionics, and high-running emotions that occur when your goal is victory, what remains after everyone has had their rant is the task of arriving at an agreement. Remind the participants at the outset that the goal is agreement and that momentary attempts at victory will only serve to delay that ultimate goal.

Summary

So there they are, the ten commandments of negotiation. If I were to add one, or two, it would destroy the symmetry of ten, which, thanks to luminaries from Moses to David Letterman, has become a widespread tradition. Instead, I conclude with a final word of encouragement that you negotiate whenever you can. Another idea that remains a part of many cultures is not to negotiate or speak up when you should. In attempting to persuade those in my midst to negotiate, I still hear the words, "I couldn't; they'd only say no." I hope the words and ideas in this book have encouraged you to stop thinking that way and worrying about whether "they'll" say no. Sometimes they'll say no; sometimes they'll say yes. At other times they'll say, "Nobody ever asked that before." Once you hear those words, know that you have *really* broken out of the pack and are well on the way to becoming a powerful negotiator. Good luck and great negotiating!

Acknowledgments

First and foremost I thank my dear friend and distinguished colleague Blanche Cook, without whose support you would not be reading these words; and my wife, Donna, for her unending encouragement and love. My thanks also to my other colleagues at John Jay College, with whom my interactions and years of friendship have meant so much, especially Eli Faber, Jerry Markowitz, Basil Wilson, Roger Witherspoon, John Stern, and Martin Wallenstein. Jeremy Travis and Jane Bowers have also been most helpful. A special note of thanks to Ron McVey, whose sage advice has always been there when I needed it. The editorial skills of Kathy Willis and the technical assistance of Melania Clavell were truly indispensable.

At Sterling Publishing I am grateful to Philip Turner for his vision and guidance, as well as Iris Blasi, Brooke Barona, Chrissy Kwasnik, Rodman Neumann, Eileen Chetti, and Rebecca Maines for their superb efforts on my behalf. The task of writing a book is small when compared with the burden of listening to the constant ruminations of the author as the work takes shape.

For their friendship and listenership along the way, I thank Bob Geline, Mike and Vicky Kay, and Erin Semler.

Index

About the Author

PATRICK COLLINS is president of Power Communication Strategies and has lectured and conducted seminars worldwide on presentation and media skills, negotiation, witness preparation, and many other communication topics. He is a professor of communications and a former department chair at John Jay College of the City University of New York. He is also the author of *Speak with Power and Confidence* (2009, available from Sterling Publishing Co., Inc.), which, in an earlier edition, was named one of the thirty best business books of 1998 by *Executive Summaries.*

Also Available

Speak with Power and Confidence:
Tested Ideas for Becoming a More Powerful Communicator
By Patrick Collins

Whether you're addressing an audience of one or one thousand, when you speak with confidence, authority, and credibility you make the kind of positive impression that people associate with a winner. In this highly focused, no-nonsense guide to transforming your speaking skills, celebrated communications consultant Patrick Collins reveals proven strategies to put you in absolute control of your image, your message, and your audience.

These are tools that everyone needs, whether standing on a podium or sitting across the desk from a job interviewer. In *Speak with Power and Confidence* you'll learn how to:

- Conquer anxiety about public speaking
- Grab your listeners' attention with your very first words
- Gain a more imposing voice and send the right nonverbal signals
- Use "command phrases" to grab and hold an audience
- Handle tough questions and tough crowds
- Deliver special-occasion speeches such as introductions, awards presentations, eulogies, and toasts
- Conduct yourself in a job interview
- Be an effective witness at trials or depositions

Having worked with thousands of clients, Patrick Collins knows that you have the potential to elevate your speaking skills to a whole new level. You owe it to yourself to get started *today*!

Sterling / 304 pages / ISBN 978-1-4027-6123-2 / $12.95 / January 2009
Available at fine bookstores everywhere

For more information, go to www.patrickjcollins.com.